Erica Brealey has practised meditation since her teens under the guidance of several well-known teachers, from whom she learned a variety of techniques. After graduating from London University with a degree in philosophy, she lived for a time on an ashram in India studying Eastern religions and philosophy, and practising yoga and meditation.

She now works as a writer and editor, and lives in North London with her husband, the publisher Nicholas Brealey, and their son Sam.

Nicholas Wilks has been practising different forms of meditation since he was at school, and ran a meditation centre as an undergraduate at Oxford, where he read English. After graduating he trained as a teacher, and subsequently studied conducting at the Royal Academy of Music. He now works as a conductor and singer.

T0316156

MEDITATION

MEDITATION

Erica Brealey
and Nicholas Wilks

Illustrated by
Maggie Raynor

1 3 5 7 9 10 8 6 4 2

Copyright © Chapters 1, 2, 3, 4, and 6, Erica Brealey 1988, 1997
Chapter 5, Erica Brealey and Nicholas Wilks 1988, 1997
Reference Section, Nicholas Wilks 1988, 1997

First published in 1998 by Macdonald Optima
This edition published in 2001 by Vermilion,
an imprint of Ebury Press, Random House,
20 Vauxhall Bridge Road, London SW1V 2SA
www.randomhouse.co.uk

Printed and bound in Great Britain by Clays Ltd, St Ives PLC

A CIP catalogue record for this book is available from the British Library.

ISBN 978 0 09 194790 3

The Random House Group Limited supports The Forest Stewardship
Council (FSC®), the leading international forest certification organisation.
Our books carrying the FSC label are printed on FSC® certified paper.
FSC is the only forest certification scheme endorsed by the leading
environmental organisations, including Greenpeace. Our
paper procurement policy can be found at
www.randomhouse.co.uk/environment

MIX
Paper | Supporting
responsible forestry
FSC
www.fsc.org
FSC® C018179

Contents

Contents

THE DALAI LAMA

FOREWORD

Nowadays people talk a great deal about the stresses of modern life and how they affect our health and happiness. As living beings, we all wish for happiness and seek to avoid suffering. One of the major factors here is our mental attitude. Physical health is closely related to our state of mind. Scientific experiments have shown that if the mind is stable and calm, basic physical functions like digestion and sleep improve. On the other hand, when someone is mentally distressed even the presence of friends, physical comfort and wealth will not make him or her happy.

Real peace and happiness come from within. The key to a happy life is to develop a calm and happy mind. If you have that, whatever the external circumstances, nothing will disturb your inner peace. A traditional way to quieten the mind, to discipline and control it, is to practice meditation.

Meditation is for everyone. Irrespective of whether you are a believer or an agnostic, a Buddhist or a Christian, proper meditation can purify your heart and mind, leading to lasting peace and happiness.

Erica Brealey and Nicholas Wilks have written this book drawing on their experience of introducing thousands of people to meditation, encouraging them to work with different techniques to find what suits them best. I have no doubt that anyone who sincerely attempts to practise meditation as it is variously described here will be rewarded with a greater sense of inner peace and strength.

June 15, 2001

Preface

As the sheer pace of life and change sends our stress levels ever higher, resulting in an epidemic of stress-related illnesses, more and more people are looking for quick fixes. But as disillusion sets in with the fads that plague the health world, word is spreading about the remarkable benefits of the ancient practice of meditation. Those who turn to meditation discover the fix that really works.

A lot of people worry that meditating may conflict with beliefs they hold or involve adopting new ones. But though it plays an important role in many Eastern religions, most forms of meditation can be practised whatever one's beliefs, and are best approached with an open mind.

Meditation radically improves mental and physical health. Amongst other things, regular meditation has been found to:

* promote deep relaxation
* relieve stress and anxiety
* lower blood pressure and heart rate
* help treat migraine, insomnia and addictions
* lift depression and improve self-esteem
* boost the immune system
* have a significant effect on ageing
* increase IQ

Enlightened medical professionals now recommend daily practice to patients suffering from stress and stress-related problems, and those who suggest it as an adjunct to conventional methods of treatment note a faster rate of improvement and recovery amongst meditators.

Meditation is, however, much more than a technique for relaxing and relieving stress. Meditation delves into the subconscious. The process of meditation is like peeling off the layers of an onion. Layers of habit and conditioning are stripped off, only to reveal more layers beneath. Gradually preconceived ideas and opinions fall away and you begin to see yourself, your relationships, and the world around you more clearly. The senses and the intellect are refined through meditation, the ability to concentrate is increased, the mind becomes clear and creativity is enhanced.

Anyone can meditate, anywhere and at any time. Above all, meditation is something you can do by yourself, for yourself. Apart from finding the time to do it, no lifestyle changes are involved, but in practice bad habits tend to slip away and meditators find themselves adopting healthier ways of life.

By devoting even ten minutes a day to meditation you will quickly notice the ripple effect spreading throughout the whole of your life and reap the benefits of improved health, inner quiet and a greater sense of wellbeing.

1

What is meditation?

Seek felicity not in your passions but in your heart. The fountain-head of happiness is not without but within.

Tolstoy, *War and Peace*

The heart is the hub of all sacred places. Go there and roam.

Bhagavan Nityananda

Seers and sages throughout history have told us to turn our attention inwards through the practice of meditation to achieve lasting fulfilment and inner peace. The techniques they have taught are tools for stilling the mind, for drawing our attention away from the outer world and immersing it in our own inner self.

There are three key aspects to the practice of meditation. The first is that we meditate not to become something, but to realize what and who we really are. The second is the paradox that although most people meditate for a reason, seeking and striving are counterproductive in actual practice. The third is the importance of having a still mind, in which thoughts are neither suppressed nor encouraged but simply witnessed.

Historically meditation has been practised for spiritual purposes but today many people take it up for purely practical reasons – for the physical and emotional benefits which are associated with regular practice, or because they find it helps them to cope effectively with the world. Meditators report increased efficiency, creativity and self-confidence, greater self-love and love for others.

What does meditation involve?

Although meditation has become much more popular in the

West in recent years, there is still a lot of confusion as to what it is and how to do it. Broadly speaking, meditation covers any of a wide range of activities from prayer to the performance of elaborate rituals, from the repetition of a word or syllable to the practice of hatha yoga, t'ai chi or Sufi dancing. Certain art forms, such as Indian music which is learnt by listening attentively to the teacher playing and getting a 'feel' for the music rather than by reading notes, are also considered forms of meditation. What these activities have in common is that they involve intuitive understanding and insight rather than rational thinking and a high degree of concentration. The attention is completely focused, the mind still but alert.

Meditation and the mind

By calling something a form of meditation we are actually saying more about the state of mind in which it is done than about the activity itself. Practising hatha yoga with concentration and awareness is a form of meditation, sitting in the lotus posture planning your evening's entertainment is not.

It is the nature of the mind to be constantly active, flitting from one thought to another. According to the great spiritual and religious teachers, it is this restlessness of the mind that lies at the root of all troubles and disease. It is only when the mind is steady and undisturbed by thoughts, feelings and emotions that we can find real peace and contentment. Only when the mind is quiet are we capable of seeing clearly, of listening totally.

Although this still, alert state of mind is particularly associated with meditation, it is a perfectly natural one experienced by everyone from time to time. Many sports involve meditative states of mind, especially those such as skiing or mountain-climbing, where a lapse of concentration can have dangerous consequences. Even ordinary everyday activities, if you really absorb yourself in them, can be forms of meditation.

Associated with a quiet mind are intuitive insights and altered states of consciousness. And, although prolonged or repeated states of heightened awareness rarely occur without meditation, they are natural phenomena which most people, in the normal course of events, experience from time to time. For example while taking a walk in the country or relaxing in the sun you may suddenly hit on the solution to something that has been puzzling you for some time. Music is widely recognized as having a powerful effect on the mind and has been used by many cultures as a way of arousing spiritual or other feelings. You can experience heightened awareness even in the middle of the most mundane activities; for example in the bath or shower you may momentarily forget everything, aware only of the feeling of the water as it flows over your skin and the way it reflects the light.

A characteristic feature of these types of insight and altered states of consciousness is that they usually happen when you are relaxed and nearly always occur at unexpected moments. Trying to repeat them by duplicating the conditions under which they occurred rarely succeeds. For example, listening to the same piece of music in the same surroundings does not necessarily result in the same state of mind.

A more reliable way of maintaining contact with such states is by the regular practice of techniques designed to still the mind – in other words, meditation.

Meditation as pure awareness

The kind of meditation which is the subject of this book is a state of pure awareness in which the mind is completely free of thoughts. It is a psychological state that you can slip into in much the same way that you drift into sleep from the waking state. What meditation really is can only be grasped by experiencing it, but awareness of the kinds of experience described above will help give you some idea of what it is like. However, whereas in the broader sense of meditation the mind is absorbed in an outer object, in the kind of meditation we are concerned with here the mind is merged within, and there is total inner stillness.

Not many people are able to enter this state of stillness immediately so various methods have been developed to bring it about. The practice of these techniques is the practice of meditation.

Techniques of meditation

Although there are innumerable techniques of meditation, they are all essentially techniques for dealing with the mind. Most forms of meditation involve focusing your attention on a specific object or task, for example staring at a candle flame, counting the breath, or repeating a simple word or phrase. Others involve the opening up of attention, maintaining awareness of whatever is going on internally and externally without comment. The meditator simply witnesses the different thoughts and images as they come and go in the mind, without making any attempt to subdue them. All of these techniques, in their different ways, help to develop concentration and gain mastery over the mind.

What meditation feels like – a trial practice

The main techniques used in meditation are described with practical instructions in Chapter 4 – you can experiment to find out which approach suits you best. But to get a feel of what meditation really is, follow the instructions below.

Meditation instructions

1. Sit upright in a comfortable position or lie down in a quiet place where you will not be disturbed

Choose a place where you will not be disturbed and take the phone off the hook. Set an alarm or timer, preferably one with a gentle ring, for 15 minutes or else place a clock where you will be able to see it without moving. Now place yourself in a comfortable position. If you are familiar with either the lotus or half lotus postures, and can remain in one of them comfortably for about 15 minutes, these are ideal positions in which to meditate. Otherwise sit cross-legged on the floor with a cushion beneath you or in a straight-backed chair without crossing your legs, in an upright position. If you are uncomfortable sitting you can lie on your back and meditate in that position. The important thing is to keep the back as straight as possible, though not rigid.

2. Relax

It helps if the body is relaxed so before beginning meditation check your body for tension and relax it if necessary. You can do this by autosuggestion, mentally instructing each part of the body in turn to relax. Close your eyes and begin with the face – it is difficult to relax the body when there is tension in the facial muscles – saying mentally 'Face relax. Eyes, relax. Jaws, relax' etc. Then continue the process with your feet, ankles, calves and so on, gradually working your way up through the rest of the body.

3. Close your eyes and focus your attention on your breathing

Sit or lie quietly with your eyes closed and become aware of your breathing. Don't disturb the natural rhythm of your breathing – just observe it as it comes in and out, without forcing anything. If thoughts, feelings or emotions arise don't worry and don't try to suppress them. If there are external noises, just let them be. When your attention wanders simply draw it back your breath, watching it as it comes in and goes out.

4. Alternatively you can try using a mantra

As an aid to meditation you can also use a mantra. A mantra is a sound, word or phrase which is repeated silently or aloud. Traditional examples of mantras are *om* (said to be the primordial sound) or *om namah shivaya* (pronounced 'om nah-mah shee-vie-yah'), but any word or sound that appeals to you can be used. It is best, though, to keep the mantra quite short – a maximum of eight or ten syllables. You can try the word 'one', or perhaps 'love' or 'peace'. If you are a Christian you might like to repeat the name of Jesus. You can even repeat your own name – Tennyson is said to have had powerful experiences by doing this. When you have chosen your mantra, repeat it silently at a normal speaking rate. If you wish, you can repeat it in rhythm with your breath – once or twice on the inhalation, once or twice on the exhalation. Immerse yourself in the mantra and become absorbed in it. Again, when thoughts and feelings arise, just let them be and gently bring your attention back to the mantra.

5. Come out of meditation gently

Never come out of meditation abruptly – you will lose many of its benefits if you do so. At the end of the session, remain in the position in which you were meditating for a few more minutes, gently moving or stretching any muscles and joints that need easing. Scan your body and mind and note the effects meditation has had. There are no 'right' effects or experiences, but meditation has both a relaxing and an energizing effect on most people. You are also likely to experience heightened awareness and sensitivity. Get up when you are ready, trying to maintain any benefits gained from meditation as long as you can.

Don't expect too much and don't worry if at first you can only keep your attention fixed for a few seconds. Almost everybody needs time to learn to meditate. Most people are unaccustomed to sitting in silence with no external distractions and it can come as a surprise to discover just how difficult it is to control the mind. An endless stream of thoughts and fantasies seems to rush into your consciousness, distracting your attention from its meditative focus. With practice, though, you will learn how to deal with these internal distractions and remain undisturbed by them.

Common misconceptions about meditation

Meditation is not reflecting on or thinking about a subject or idea

Meditation and thinking things over are completely different activities, although thoughts may arise during the practice of meditation. In fact learning how to let go of one's thoughts is part of the process of learning to meditate. This does not mean driving them away, which is unlikely to succeed, but simply allowing them to come and go, without pursuing them, interfering with them or getting caught up in them. In deep meditation all thought ceases.

Meditation is not a form of hypnosis

Hypnosis, whether self-induced or induced by a third party, is a form of trance in which the subject has suspended to some degree his or her normal self-control and critical faculties, and is in a passive and highly receptive state. The importance of this trance state is that, while in it, the subject is open to suggestions and instructions that the conscious self would block. In this state the subject can be persuaded to modify his or her behaviour or beliefs in specific ways, for example to give up smoking. This is done by a process of suggestion involving either a third party or, in the case of self-hypnosis, the use of tape recordings, printed cards and so on. Certain thoughts are encouraged and made to predominate over others.

In meditation no process of suggestion is involved and no one thought is given predominance over another, so the question of hypnotism does not arise. Meditation is not a form of trance and it does not mean losing consciousness. It is a state of full awareness in which the mind is still but fully alert and in which the meditator is completely focused on the present moment.

Meditation does not involve beliefs or value systems

A major misconception about meditation which discourages many otherwise interested people from taking up the practice is the idea that it involves the adoption of particular religious or philosophical beliefs, or that it may conflict with religious beliefs already held.

It is true that there are many groups and religious movements in which meditation is taught against a background system of beliefs. However, meditation can be practised either in a secular or a religious context and it does not in any way require acceptance of a set of beliefs. On the contrary, meditation should be approached with an open mind, and all beliefs and concepts set aside as far as possible during the actual period of meditation.

Meditation is something you do for yourself and, generally speaking, by yourself. It is a process in which you gradually come to know and understand yourself more fully.Therefore whether or not the technique chosen is associated within the context of a particular religion – and most can be traced back to one or other of the mythical traditions – meditation remains a highly individual practice. The ultimate goal of meditation has nothing to do with accepting a system of beliefs. It is a direct and very personal experience of one's own true nature.

2

Why meditate?

There is now widespread recognition, backed up by the results of scientific research, of the beneficial effects that meditation has on mental and physical health. This explains the increasing popularity of meditation in the West today, and the psychophysiological changes associated with meditation are discussed later in this chapter. But in most Eastern countries where meditation is practised, as well as for many Westerners who have taken it up, health benefits are still secondary to the traditional goal – mystical experience.

Mystical experience

Meditation has been practised as a means to spiritual development for thousands of years. Through the process of meditation your awareness is gradually refined and expanded, and your understanding of yourself and your relationship to the world around you deepens. The ultimate goal of meditation is direct experiential knowledge of the true nature of reality.

The underlying reality apprehended through mystical experience is known by many different names. Philosophers call it ultimate or absolute reality, poets and visionaries sometimes refer to it as the One or the Truth. It is the Tao or Way of Taoists, the Beloved of the Sufis and the Void of Buddhists. Christian mystics know it as the Godhead and Hindus as Brahman or the Self.

During mystical experience all sense of 'I' and 'mine' dissolves. Individual consciousness merges into pure, unlimited being. This is not a confused state, but one of great clarity. Many different terms have been used to describe it – pure being, supreme consciousness, ecstatic bliss, infinite love, the union of opposites, undifferentiated 'suchness', and so on – but these names and descriptions convey little. According to all mystics, the truth can only be realized experientially. Language can never adequately describe it. Aware of the limitations of language, mystics have used myths, metaphors, allegories, imagery and paradoxes to communicate their experience and transmit their knowledge. Studies of these make it clear that the experience of mystics of all times and all places is essentially the same, although details may differ and interpretations vary. The central feature that all emphasize is the fundamental unity and interrelationship of all things. This is a dynamic unity, however – ever flowing, ever changing and ever spontaneous.

No one who has had repeated mystical experience doubts its validity. Even a momentary glimpse of the truth can have a transforming effect. The direct experience of reality, and the knowledge arising from it, lie at the heart of all mysticism. The goal of meditation is to become established in this knowledge and the inner teaching of all religions and mystical traditions aims at this.

Parallels between mysticism and modern physics

The view of reality emerging from recent developments in physics is, in essence, very similar to that taught by all mystics. Both the theory of relativity and quantum theory are leading us towards an organic, holistic view of reality. This is in stark contrast to the view of classical physics, which is based on dualism and holds a mechanistic view of nature. The concepts discussed in this section may be difficult for anyone without much scientific knowledge, but the parallels between reality as it is experienced by mystics and the reality demonstrated by modern physicists are so striking, and their consequences so important in the area of health and healing, that they cannot be ignored.

The Cartesian–Newtonian model of the universe

Western thought since the seventeenth century has been tremendously influenced by the work of the French philosopher René Descartes, often regarded as the founder of modern philosophy. Through a process of radical doubt Descartes arrived at his famous statement *'Cogito, ergo sum'*, 'I think, therefore I am'. From this statement he built up his entire philosophy, dividing mind and matter into two separate and totally independent realms. This has led people in the West to identify themselves with their minds rather than with their entire being, since, according to the prevailing view, the body belonged to the material universe and so was nothing but a machine. The consequences of this dualistic view have been very apparent in the field of medicine.

Descartes's dualism, with its mechanistic view of nature, also had great influence in the sphere of science. It provided the conceptual framework for the mechanistic model of the universe constructed by the English scientist Isaac Newton, upon which classical physics is founded. The basic elements (atoms) in the Newtonian model of the universe are small, solid, indestructible particles from which all matter is composed. In this system, all physical events are reduced to the movement, caused by the force of gravity, of these particles in time and space according to fixed laws of motion.

The Newtonian model was regarded as the ultimate theory of physical phenomena and the basis of all science until the end of the nineteenth century when new discoveries such as electric and magnetic phenomena, which could not be described by the mechanistic model, made its limitations apparent. However it was not until the sensational scientific developments of the early twentieth century that scientists were forced to accept a radically different view of reality.

Modern physics

Modern physics begins with the work of Einstein at the beginning of this century. His first great contribution to physics lay in his special theory of relativity. According to this theory, time and space are not absolute, independent entities. They are insepara-bly connected, forming a four-dimensional continuum. An important consequence of this is that mass is shown to be nothing but a form of energy.

Einstein's second great contribution lay in a new way of looking at electromagnetic phenomena. This played an influential part in the development of quantum theory, a theory which has completely destroyed the classical notion of solid objects. According to quantum theory there are no hard, solid particles forming the basic building blocks of the universe as assumed in classical physics. Even subatomic particles are nothing like this.

They are abstract entities appearing sometimes like waves and sometimes like particles, depending on how we look at them. Subatomic particles are not things at all but are interconnections between things, which in turn are interconnections between other things. They do not exist with certainty in specific places, but only show tendencies to exist. This means that the material objects with which we are familiar in everyday life are, at the subatomic level, wave-like patterns of probability. What gives matter its solid aspect is the fact that, when confined to a small space, the electrons in an atom move around the nucleus much faster, making the atom appear as a rigid sphere.

An important feature of quantum theory is that the characteristics of atomic phenomena depend upon the consciousness of the human observer. Whether an electron appears as a wave or a particle is a function of the interaction between the electron and the observer. The electron does not, in fact, have any objective properties at all. This means that Cartesian dualism – the theory that reality consists of two independent and fundamental principles, mind and matter – can no longer be upheld. Mind and matter, man and nature are inextricably connected. We are all part of one another.

Thus the study of the atomic and subatomic world is demonstrating that the entire world is interconnected, interrelated and interdependent. The constituents of matter are not isolated entities, but integral parts of an inseparable whole which includes human consciousness as an essential part. Physicists have discovered the fundamental oneness of the universe by means of abstract mathematical formulae and the indirect observation of subatomic phenomena, using highly sensitive scientific instruments. Mystics experience it directly in the heightened states of consciousness reached in deep meditation.

Awareness of this unity does not mean that mystics and physicists no longer recognize the individuality of the objects and events which occur in the phenomenal world of our everyday experience. It is simply that they do not see the differences and contrasts of the world as a fundamental feature of reality.

Conventional and holistic approaches to health

The consequences of the classical world view, which divided mind and matter into two separate and totally independent realms, have been very apparent in the field of health. Conventional medicine in the West has viewed the body as a machine, parts of which must be repaired or replaced when they break down. These different parts are treated by different specialists, often with little regard to the rest of the organism. Although Western medicine has become highly skilled at treating the physical symptoms of disease, it has given little attention to the part played by mental processes and emotional attitudes, as well as by social and environmental factors, in the causation of disease.

Modern surgical techniques and the development of chemotherapy, the major tools of conventional medicine, have saved countless lives as well as alleviating much pain and distress. These tools are also used in the medical treatment of mental disorders, and can be remarkably effective in controlling symptoms. However drugs often have toxic side-effects, resulting in further complications, and may even be counter-effective. For example in the case of mental illness, medication suppresses symptoms but does not cure, because it does not address the psychological roots of the disorder. In the long term, this can only be counter-therapeutic. For all the miraculous achievements of modern medicine, its narrow, mechanistic view of the human body is a serious flaw. Furthermore, its methods of treatment all too often ignore the patient's own powers of self-healing and responsibility for his or her state of health.

Alternative approaches to health and healing, such as acupuncture or homoeopathy, take a view which is much more consistent with the picture of reality emerging from the new physics and as perceived by mystics. These approaches are often termed 'holistic', from the Greek *holos* (whole), because they view the individual as an integrated whole, all the parts of which are interconnected and interdependent. No part can be damaged or removed without affecting the whole. Alternative therapies recognize the connection between mind, body and spirit, and take into account the way mental and physical states interact and affect each another. Illness is thus viewed as a disorder or imbalance of the whole person, rather than as something caused by a single factor, such as a malfunction of a particular part of the physical body.

There are various methods of holistic treatment, but most involve very subtle interference with the organism designed to stimulate the natural process of self-healing, as opposed to the interventionist techniques of conventional medicine. And in contrast to the orthodox system of treating illness, which delegates all responsibility to the doctor, a holistic approach requires the individual to take personal responsibility for the treatment and prevention of disease by adopting a healthy lifestyle – wholefoods, physical exercise, relaxation and meditation. There is now scientific evidence for the psychophysiological benefits of meditation, primarily due to its role in alleviating stress.

Stress

So much has been said and written about stress in recent times that most of us are aware of it and have some idea of what it is. However the term is used very loosely, and tends to be associated only with situations and circumstances which cause discomfort and distress.

What is stress?

The term 'stress' was originally used in physics to describe a force which acts on an object, producing or tending to produce deformation or strains within it. It is also used to describe the state of an object under such conditions. The extent to which the object is strained or deformed by the force acting on it will depend upon its load-bearing capacity, flexibility and tolerance. If the object returns to its original shape or form after removing the force it is said to be elastic, whereas if it remains deformed it is said to be plastic. So if you stretch an elastic band and then release it, it will return to its original shape. But if you stretch it too far, it will remain permanently stretched even after the force is removed, or it may snap.

Applied to living organisms, stress is a state of psychophysiological arousal in response to social, physical and emotional factors, in particular those which constitute a threat or which requires change or adaptation. The biochemical changes which accompany this response, sometimes referred to as the 'fight or flight response', are described on pages 19–21. The term 'stress' can also be used to refer to the forces or circumstances that act on the organism and cause this response.

Stress as a necessary ingredient of life

Stress is generally thought of as a dark threatening cloud hanging over people's lives which should be avoided at all costs. But temporary stress is, in fact, an essential aspect of life without which people could not cope effectively with their environment. For example the biological stress mechanism is fundamental to the realization of the most basic of human drives – procreation and survival. Athletes must be nervous before a race to perform at their best. Stress responses such as getting anxious before making an important decision, being tense before performing in public or feeling frightened when confronted with danger are all perfectly natural. They are part of the body's normal adaptive reaction to challenging situations and enable the individual to deal with them in the most effective way.

Stress is present in all activity and without it there would be no change, no creativity and no spice to life. People would be unable to meet any of the demands made on them and there would be no opportunity for personal growth. It is only when stress is prolonged or excessive, and the energy generated by the stress response is not discharged, that it becomes harmful and a significant factor in the development of disease.

What causes stress?

A wide varity of stimuli can trigger the stress response. Major life crises such as bereavement, divorce, financial problems or examinations are obvious sources of stress. Others which affect everyone to some degree include environmental and social factors such as air and noise pollution, urban overcrowding, living and working conditions. Work problems are among the most common and intense stress triggers. The frustration and dissatisfaction caused by jobs which do not demand enough, repetitious tasks or sheer boredom can be as stressful as deadlines, pressures, too much responsibility or too much competition. Other factors which can contribute to stress include relationships, socio-economic status, the rate of change in people's lives, and lack of sleep.

What is less commonly realized is the fact that pleasurable events such as holidays, love affairs or promotion can also be stressful. Stress is an integral part of life and cannot be avoided. Elimination of the major sources might easily involve changes of partner, family, friends, job and philosophy of life – changes which, for most people, are neither feasible nor desirable. What can be done, however, is to control the amount of stress in one's life and prevent the overload which can result in serious damage to the organism.

Stress overload

Stress expert Dr Malcolm Carruthers likens stress to an electric current in a circuit. The circuit is designed to have a certain amount of electricity flowing through it, without which it cannot function. But if the current is too strong and the circuit is overloaded, it will overheat or blow a fuse. Similarly a person whose stress tolerance is exceeded, or who handles it inappropriately, will get hot and bothered or 'blow a fuse'. As in a machine, the weakest link will go first, whether it's a cardiac fuse that leads to a heart attack, or a stomach fuse that causes an ulcer. Some people blow a mental fuse and have a nervous breakdown. People vary tremendously in their tolerance to stress and while some people, such as politicians, may thrive on and enjoy high levels of stress, others 'blow a fuse' at the slightest irritation.

Indications that stress has reached harmful levels may be emotional, behavioural or physiological. No two people share an identical set of symptoms, but typical emotional reactions to stress are an inability to concentrate, difficulty in making decisions, feelings of low self-esteem, depression, fear, anxiety, irritability and emotional outbursts. Common behavioural symptoms are increased smoking and drinking, an increase or decrease in appetite, social withdrawal, and physical mannerisms such as grinding the teeth, biting the nails, tapping the feet and so on. Physiological indications include tension headaches, hypertension, insomnia, irregular breathing, palpitations and diarrhoea. Fortunately, there are effective ways in which excessive stress can be alleviated and stress levels prevented from building up to uncomfortable or dangerous levels.

Fight or flight response

The biochemical response which is triggered by any stress signal, whether real or imaginary, physical or psychological, is known as the 'fight or flight' response'. This response is much the same in human beings as in other animals, and involves a complex series of biochemical reactions which, as the phrase suggests, prepare the organism for intense activity – physical fight or physical flight.

When the fight or flight response comes into operation, the stress hormones adrenaline and noradrenaline are immediately released into the system, rapidly followed by the hormone cortisol, resulting in a number of changes in the body. The lungs take in more oxygen, the heart beats faster and blood pressure rises. The circulation of blood to the muscles of the limbs and brain is increased, enabling clear thinking, quick action and quick decision making. At the same time the liver releases sugars and fatty acids into the bloodstream to provide energy for the muscles. The muscles become tense in preparation for action and the body prepares to keep itself cool by increased perspiration. Body procresses that will not be needed, such as digestion, cease as blood is diverted away from the skin and digestive organs. The bowel and bladder muscles relax, which can produce a desire to defecate or urinate.

In this state of arousal, a person is in the best condition to cope with challenge or danger. Once action has been taken by fighting or fleeing and the danger has passed, the organs relax and the body reverts to its normal state of balance, or homeostasis.

Healthy and injurious responses

Our bodies respond in virtually the same way to any stress signal, in common with all mammals confronted with a potential threat. If startled by a sudden noise or movement, the fight-flight response immediately comes into play and even a sleeping dog will be on its feet in a split second, hackles raised, alert and ready to fight or take flight. Either way, the energy released by the stress hormones is metabolised and, once the danger has passed, the animal can rest and relax.

The fight or flight response was very well suited to early humans, whose survival depended upon their physical ability to fight or to escape. But modern-day survival, at least in the West, is more a question of competing for and holding on to jobs, meeting production deadlines, successful negotiating and so on. The problem is that this psychological stress results in a physical response. If you get held up in a traffic jam and miss an appointment, or you lose an important business contract, the fight or flight response is simply inappropriate. You can neither escape nor physically assault your 'opponent', though you might feel the urge to. If no socially acceptable action is open to you, the energy generated by the stress response is not used up. The body remains in a state of imbalance and you feel 'wound up'. Furthermore, unlike animals, we tend to carry on thinking about whatever is worrying or upsetting us. This inability to switch off keeps our stress levels raised. The result is prolonged or chronic stress which is highly damaging to health.

While the stress response is a healthy adaptive reaction, it evolved as a temporary state to deal with emergencies. In practice, unfortunately, the fight or flight response does not occur only in emergency situations, and it is the repeated biological false alarms which lead to damage. To try to understand the difference between healthy and injurious stress responses, imagine that you were crossing the road and a car started to accelerate towards you, threatening to run you over. In a matter of seconds your heart rate would practically double and you would break into a run almost instantly. Once you had reached the other side of the road safely, you would probably heave a sigh of relief and experience exhilaration and a trembling sensation in your body as you began to breathe normally again and to relax. Compare this reaction with the way you feel at the end of a stressful day when there has been no time to recover between one particular demand or crisis and the next. Your body is likely to have been in a state of perpetual arousal throughout the day. It is this prolonged stress which is responsible for the development of stress-related disorders. If the body is not released from this reactive state – whether because the energy created by it is not used up, because the perceived 'threat' persists, or because the response is repeatedly triggered – then disease is the likely outcome.

Stress and ill health

When the stress response is prolonged and no physical action is taken to release the organism from this state, numerous undesirable consequences follow. For example, the fatty acids released into the bloodstream to provide energy are deposited on the walls of the arteries, leading in the long term to arteriosclerosis and heart failure. High levels of hydrochloric acid in the stomach may cause severe indigestion and ultimately result in peptic ulcers. There is no space in this book to go into more details, but stress is recognized as the principal cause of hypertension, migraine and insomnia, and is strongly implicated as a factor in many other illnesses, the major ones being cancer, arthritis and respiratory diseases, such as bronchitis and emphy-. sema.

But the effects are not manifested on a purely physical level. Neurotic and psychotic disorders may result, or destructive forms of behaviour such as drug abuse or crime. The consequences of this for society as a whole are apparent. On an individual level, anyone who has had experience of living or working at close quarters with someone who is under a great deal of pressure – and most people have – knows just how difficult this can be and how easy it is to be affected by it. Disturbing evidence has also recently been produced indicating that pre-natal stress suffered by mothers-to-be could affect their babies, causing them to develop more slowly and have more difficulty in coping with pressures and conflicts.

The list of stress-related disorders is endless. Even the most conservative sources estimate that well over half of the disorders treated by general practitioners are psychosomatic or stress-related. Some estimates put this figure as high as 90 per cent. Many medical experts believe that prolonged stress also produces increased susceptibility to viral and other infections, traditionally classified as non-psychosomatic, by weakening the immune system. Vaccination, antibiotics and improved living conditions have effectively eliminated or controlled devastating infectious diseases such as smallpox, typhoid, cholera and polio, although some infectious diseases, such as tuberculosis, have developed strains resistant to antibiotics and are on the increase again. Today, the major killers in the more industrially developed countries are cardiovascular disorders and cancer. These diseases, often described as diseases of civilization, are stress-related.

Even taking a conservative view of the role played by stress in the causing of disease and other forms of ill health, it is clear that learning how to handle stress is probably the single most important step an individual can take towards positive health and longevity. This is not to say that all stress can or should be eliminated, nor is it to suggest that we should all always enjoy perfect health all of the time. Periods of illness or crises can also be periods of profound personal transformation, bringing about very positive changes in lifestyle and philosophy. We simply need to find ways of preventing stress from building up to dangerous levels. Some may find that vigorous physical activity is a sufficient antidote, but most people need to adopt conscious relaxation techniques which effectively 'switch off' the fight or flight response.

Meditation – the relaxation response

The physiological and biochemical changes in the body which occur in response to stress are regulated by the two branches of the autonomic nervous system – the sympathetic and the parasympathetic. The fight or flight response is the result of sympathetic nervous activity, which is triggered initially by a stress signal. When the danger has passed or the challenge has been met, the parasympathetic system is activated producing a response which is the reverse of the fight or flight response. The heart rate decreases and blood pressure is lowered, breathing slows down and less oxygen is taken in, the muscles relax and digestion continues.

As already explained, serious health problems can arise as a consequence of prolonged sympathetic arousal. Meditation counteracts this state of arousal by activating the parasympathetic response, which has also been termed 'the relaxation response'. There has been considerable research into the effects of meditation, most of which has been conducted with Zen masters, Indian yogis, and more recently with Western practitioners of Transcendental Meditation (TM). These studies have demonstrated that meditation is accompanied by:

- a significant decrease in heart rate and a lowering or stabilization of blood pressure
- slower, shallower breathing, and reduced oxygen consumption
- a decrease in skin conductivity associated with reduction in anxiety (when people are anxious or nervous they tend to perspire more, which decreases skin resistance to an electric current. Increases in perspiration too slight to be visible to the naked eye can be detected by machines designed to measure electrical resistance, and it is this principle that is used in lie detectors).

- changes in brain-wave activity indicating a relaxed but alert state (see Meditation and the Brain, pages 25–26).

Meditation can, therefore, be used to 'switch off' the fight or flight response. (It should, however, be noted that while most kinds of meditation – and all those for which instructions are given in this book – will induce a state of relaxation, the techniques used in some systems, such as kundalini yoga, can involve states of high arousal.) The beneficial effects are not confined to the period of meditation, but carry over into the rest of the day, enabling regular meditators to cope more efficiently with the pressures of everyday life.

Physiological arousal and recovery in meditators

It might at first be inferred from these findings that meditation leads to a lack of reactivity and responsiveness. This would, of course, be quite undesirable for a number of different reasons. For one, physiological arousal is a vital response in a dangerous situation where swift reactions may be needed. For another, the traditional goals of meditation are towards increased sensitivity and perception, not dullness and inertia.

Because the gathering of scientific evidence requires the presence of research workers and the use of measuring instruments, it is virtually impossible to acquire data on the performance of meditators in real-life situations. However there is evidence to show that meditators do, in fact, experience higher levels of arousal where appropriate. In one study a group of experienced meditators and a control group were shown a highly stressful film which was originally made to impress upon woodworkers the importance of following safety procedures. The film depicts three accidents, one fatal, caused by ignoring these procedures. As predicted, skin conductivity and heart rate rose and fell in direct response to the incidents shown in the film in both groups. The most interesting result, however, was entirely unanticipated. The meditators showed significantly greater increases in skin conductivity and heart rate just before each stressful incident, but also made a far quicker recovery following the incidents. This suggests that meditators have a greater range of response than non-meditators, and increased sensitivity.

Habituation to repeated or continuous stress stimuli

Related to this pattern of arousal and recovery is the phenomenon known as habituation. If an individual is subjected to a repeated or continuous stress situation – for example extreme overcrowding or a loud, unpleasant noise from a road drill – the stress response will slowly diminish. This ability to habituate to repeated and unavoidable stimuli in the environment is essential. Inability to do so leads to stress-related disorders. Again, experimental evidence, in which experienced meditators and control groups have been subjected to prolonged or repeated noxious noises, indicates that meditators have a more rapid recovery rate than non-meditators and are more able to cope with and adapt to their environment.

Meditation and the brain

Even more interesting than the effects of meditation on the body are its effects on the mind, but this is an area in which we have to rely more on personal accounts and observations than scientific data. However, general patterns of brain activity can be measured, albeit somewhat crudely, by an instrument called an electroencephalograph (EEG). Studies using this instrument show patterns of activity during meditation that are distinct from either the normal waking or sleep patterns of activity.

An electroencephalograph measures electric currents in the brain, which are correlated with different mental states, by means of electrodes placed on the scalp. Brain-wave activity is classified into alpha, beta, delta or theta activity according to the frequency of the electrical patterns recorded. Delta activity is the slowest, at 0.5 to 4 cycles per second, and is associated with deep sleep. Theta activity consists of patterns of between 4 and 8 cycles per second and corresponds to drowsiness, daydreaming or the dream state. Alpha activity, on which most interest has been centred, ranges from 8 to 13 cycles per second and predominates when an individual is in a relaxed but alert state. Most people can move from an aroused state to a state in which alpha brain-wave activity is predominant simply by closing their eyes and relaxing, but it is unusual to be able to maintain predominant alpha with the eyes open. Beta activity, at 13 cycles per second and above, up to around 30 or 40 cycles per second, predominates during normal waking consciousness.

In all studies on meditators alpha activity appears, with or without other patterns of brain-wave activity, but different readings have been obtained in different studies. It is likely that these vary according to the length of time that subjects have been practising meditation and to the type of meditation practised. The general picture that seems to emerge is that initially, on beginning a period of meditation, there is a shift towards more alpha activity. Later in meditation there may also be some theta activity, especially in the case of experienced meditators. During deep meditation, however, there are bursts of very high frequency beta activity between 20 and 40 cycles per second, even as high as 50 cycles per second. At the end of meditation alpha activity reappears and may persist even with the eyes open.

Another interesting feature is that alpha brain-wave activity during meditation appears to spread from the back of the brain, whereas alpha readings are usually found to cover the entire scalp, building up first in the left hemisphere of the brain and then in the right to present a symmetrical pattern. This is in contrast to the patterns shown normally by most people. It is now known that each hemisphere of the brain has a different function to perform, the left side being concerned with language, analytical thinking and so on, while the right side has to do with images and patterns, creative thinking etc. Western society has tended to place more importance on rational thinking with the result that, in most people, brain-wave activity predominates in the left hemisphere. This is in contrast to artistically minded people, who generally show predominantly right-hemisphere activity. Although the findings of research into the brain-wave patterns of meditators are not yet fully understood, it appears that meditation acts to restore the balance between right- and left-hemisphere activity, and also to widen the range of activity into areas of the brain previously lying dormant.

Meditation as therapy

The psychophysiological correlates of meditation described above are clear evidence of its beneficial effects on mental and physical health. Additionally, although major lifestyle changes are not inherent in the practice of meditation, regular meditators tend to adopt a more positive outlook and a healthier lifestyle.

This includes reduced consumption of caffeine, nicotine, alcohol and other non-prescription drugs, adoption of a healthier diet – usually eating less meat and less refined or processed foods – and a more regular routine. Whether these changes are the result of meditation itself or of self-selection in becoming a meditator is not clear, but there is no doubt that they contribute to the overall ability of meditators to cope better with stress. And whether improvements observed in subjects whose clinical treatment includes meditation are the result of lifestyle changes or meditation *per se* is also a matter for debate, but ultimately the fact of improvement is of more importance to both doctor and patient than isolating the specific cause of the improvement.

Increasing application is indeed being found for meditation in a clinical setting. It has been used successfully as a therapy in the treatment of hypertension, insomnia and drug abuse. It has also been used effectively in the treatment of cancer. As preventative therapy it is likely to reduce the incidence of all these conditions and of a whole range of other disorders including migraine, ulcers, heart attacks and arthritis. Improvements in mental health resulting from regular practice of meditation include decreased anxiety, irritability, depression and neuroses, and increased calmness, emotional stability and self-control. A significant number of psychiatrists and psychotherapists are also beginning to use meditation as an adjunct to conventional methods of treatment. There is no objective scientific evidence available which proves the efficacy of meditation as an aid to psychotherapeutic techniques, but therapists report a much faster rate of improvement among meditators. This is probably in part due to reduction in stress and in part to the mental purification, discussed below, that occurs as part of the process of meditation.

The process of meditation

There is a Zen saying that the journey is more important than the destination. Traditionally, as discussed at the beginning of the chapter, the goal or 'destination' of meditation has been full spiritual development and the realization of one's greatest potential, but for most people this is unrealistic and remote. More important is the process of personal transformation involved in moving towards this goal – the process of self-discovery and the mental, physical and emotional purification that result from regular meditation.

The first effects observed on taking up meditation are usually physical – a feeling of deep relaxation as tension is released from the body. This is often accompanied by a feeling of 'coming home', of returning to the centre of one's being. As your meditation develops, however, it can come as an unwelcome surprise to find unwanted thoughts, fantasies, obsessions and other distractions forcing their way into your consciousness and disturbing your concentration. Feelings such as anger and hatred may also arise with a great intensity. Many people, unfortunately, become discouraged at this point and give up. Often they do not realize that this is an inevitable part of the process of inner purification.

Just as toxins are released as a result of physical purification – for example if you go on a fast or give up tea or coffee – producing unpleasant withdrawal symptoms such as headaches, so mental and emotional 'toxins' are released during meditation. This is due to the release of repressed emotions, the resolving of deep conflicts, dealing with unfinished psychic material and so on. In this sense the results of meditation are similar to those aimed for in psychoanalysis. However while psychoanalytic techniques are purposely designed to bring back to conscious awareness traumatic or repressed events, meditation is a completely natural process in which no conscious attempt is made to relive past experiences. The process of purification brought about by meditation is nothing to worry about, but it can be quite difficult and there is no doubt that the help and guidance of an experienced teacher can be invaluable at this stage.

The process of meditation involves the gradual penetration and removal of the layers of conditioning that hide a person's true self and cloud his or her perception of the world. As preconceived ideas and judgements are abandoned, one's awareness of the world and one's relationship to it becomes clearer. And, as the senses and understanding are refined, and powers of concentration develop, thinking becomes clearer and creativity is enhanced.

Though many generalizations may be made, each meditator has different experiences according to his or her particular temperament and needs. Meditation is a private and personal process through which your perception of the world and your entire being are gradually transformed.

Meditation – a holistic phenomenon

Scientific research has provided evidence of the beneficial effects of meditation on physical and mental health, but meditation also has a profound effect on the individual's personality and general quality of life. By turning the attention within, meditation leads to greater familiarity with the inner world of thoughts and feelings and to increased self-knowledge. By increasing the power of concentration, greater control and efficiency are achieved in all areas of life. Meditators claim to feel more at peace, more centred, more balanced and more aware. They have greater enthusiasm and vitality and a stronger sense of their own potential. They feel more at one with the world.

Everyone who meditates has their own personal reasons for doing so. Many people take it up for the sake of the beneficial effects it has on overall health and state of mind, although as meditation deepens these goals may change. Whatever the original reasons may be, however, the holistic effects of meditation will be experienced by anyone who practises regularly.

3

Establishing the practice

While the actual period of meditation can be very uplifting and inspiring, what happens at any one particular session is less important than the general effect it has on your life. Just as fitness is achieved and maintained only by regular exercise and a balanced diet, lasting results from meditation can be obtained only by regular practice. Establishing a routine and developing good habits of posture, breathing, and so on from the very beginning are a tremendous support to the practice of meditation, and of equal importance to the choice of techniques, which is discussed in Chapter 4.

The idea is not, however, to become dependent on a set procedure. On the contrary, once you have established your practice by meditating in a systematic manner, according to a schedule, you will be able to meditate anywhere and at any time.

Where to meditate

Just as a beautiful temple or church where people have spent time in prayer and contemplation has a calming and soothing influence on all who enter it, so, given a little thought and preparation, a place in the home set aside especially for the purpose can create a similar effect, acting as a stimulus to meditation.

Choose a quiet, pleasant place where you will not be disturbed by noise, people or other distractions. The ideal arrangement, if possible, is to set aside a room, or corner of a room, and reserve it solely for meditation. Use the same place regularly, especially in the early stages – the associations and the atmosphere that builds up will make it easy to slip into meditation whenever you sit there. If noise is a problem, earplugs can be useful. If there is a telephone in the room, unplug it or take it off the hook. Ensure that there is adequate heating and that you are as comfortable as possible – the more comfortable you are the more easily you will be able to concentrate on your practice, and the more likely you will be to continue with it. Wear light, loose-fitting clothes and remove your shoes.

Simple, attractive surroundings are helpful for settling into a meditative state, so anything you can do to make your place of meditation pleasing to the eye or other senses is effort well spent. Avoid harsh lighting – natural light or low, diffuse lighting are more relaxing. Some people like to meditate in the dark, or by the light of a candle, as they find it helps them to turn their attention inwards.

Remember, though, when preparing a place of meditation, to consider the feelings of the people you live with. Candlelight and burning incense can be a powerful means of creating atmosphere and mood, but if you live with someone who is allergic to incense or unsympathetic towards meditation, set about your meditation with the minimum of fuss. In any case, you should never allow any kind of aid to meditation to becoming indispensable. If you feel unable to meditate unless you have a particular object, picture or other paraphernalia about you, break the habit. Meditation should lead to inner freedom, not greater dependence.

When to meditate and for how long

It is not essential to establish set times of day for meditation but, generally speaking, it is best to set yourself a realistic programme when you take up meditation and stick to it as far as possible, without becoming obsessive about it.

Ideally you should meditate twice a day for a fixed length of time. Many teachers and traditions consider sunrise and sunset to be the best times for meditation. First thing in the morning is, in fact, an excellent time for most people. When you awake your mind is relatively clear, whereas later on it may take a while to turn your attention away from the events and preoccupations of the day. Other good times to try are before your evening meal or before going to sleep, provided these times fit in with your family and daily routine. Whatever time or times you choose, it is not a good idea to meditate just after eating – the body is busy digesting the meal, and you are likely to be less alert. Allow an hour or two after a light meal and longer after a heavier one, and leave as long a period of time as you can in between meditation sessions if you practise twice a day.

It is best to build up the length of time for which you meditate gradually, rather than set yourself targets which will be hard to keep. Beginners are recommended to sit for a minimum of 10 minutes and a maximum of 30, but it is better to spend just 5 minutes a day regularly than a longer period very erratically. Don't worry if nothing seems to be happening – the mere fact of remaining in a still posture for a fixed time is in itself beneficial, so stay seated or lying down for whatever length of time you have set yourself. Keeping a close watch on time is not, of course, conducive to meditation, but if you regularly meditate at the same time each day you will soon find that your body becomes accustomed to the routine and you will not need a clock to let you know when the time is up. Until you get used to judging time, however, put a clock where you can see it easily or set an alarm – avoid one with a shrill bell or else muffle it with a cushion – to mark the end of your meditation period.

Posture

The posture in which you meditate should be conducive to a still, relaxed, but alert frame of mind. This does not mean you need to sit in the classic lotus posture in which each foot is placed over the opposite thigh – sheer torture for the average Westerner who has not practised yoga. Even though you may find it worthwhile making the effort to master one of the cross-legged positions described below, you will achieve nothing by forcing your body into a position you find painful or unnatural.

The best posture for meditation is one in which you can comfortably sit still with your back straight for about half an hour. If your posture is firm and still, your mind will automatically become steady. Holding the back as straight as you can, although not in a rigid way, and with the stomach muscles relaxed, is considered very important in meditation. Such a position will allow you to sit comfortably for a long period and help you to stay attentive and alert. It also reduces stress and fatigue by allowing the blood to flow freely round the body. In some systems, such as yoga, keeping the spine erect is also claimed to have spiritual benefits, because it allows the 'subtle' energy currents to flow more easily.

Certain movements may occasionally take place in meditation. Begin by sitting in the correct posture, but if your head nods or sways in meditation, do not resist the movement – unless, of course, it is due to falling asleep or laziness.

Any of the following postures are suitable for meditation. A firm cushion or mat under the buttocks can be used for ease and comfort if you are sitting in one of the cross-legged positions. Because they are classical meditation positions, the lotus posture and perfect posture are described first. However most people will be more comfortable in the easy posture or sitting on a chair. If you are uncomfortable sitting, you can lie on the floor in the *shavasana* ('corpse pose') to meditate. This position is very easy and very relaxing, the only drawback being that it is also very easy to fall asleep while in it.

Lotus posture (padmasana)

The lotus posture, in which the Buddha is frequently depicted, is ideal for meditation. The legs are locked together, providing a firm base from which the meditator will neither topple over nor fall asleep, and no effort is required to maintain the position.

Lotus posture

Once the knees and ankles have become sufficiently flexible to hold the posture easily, it is a very relaxing pose. However, for anyone used only to sitting on a chair, it will be very painful in the knee area to begin with and it may be a long time before the position feels comfortable.

It is advisable to loosen up the joints of the hips, knees and ankles with the preparatory exercises described below before attempting to sit in the lotus posture and then gradually to build up the time you sit in it – one minute to start with, then two, and so on. Never force your legs into this position, as this could cause serious damage.

Preparatory exercises

1. Sit on the floor with your legs stretched out in front of you. Bend the right knee and grasp the right ankle and foot with

Exercise 1

both hands, placing the right ankle on the left leg just above the knee, with the right foot extending beyond the leg. Keeping the foot, ankle and calf relaxed, hold the right leg just above the ankle with the right hand and, using the left hand, rotate the right foot first in one direction, then in the other. Repeat ten times in each direction, then change legs and repeat the exercise.

2. Sit on the floor as in Exercise 1, bend the right knee and place the ankle on the left leg just above the knee. Keeping the right leg completely relaxed, grasp the right ankle with both hands, lift it above the leg and shake the loose foot vigorously. Change legs and repeat the exercise.

Exercise 2

3. Sit on the floor as in Exercise 1, bend the right knee, and place the right foot on the left leg. With the left hand holding the foot and the right hand wrapped round the leg, holding the ankle, lift the leg as high as you can. Keeping your back and head straight, describe large circles with the foot, bringing it towards the body at the top of the circle and away at the bottom. Repeat ten times with one leg and then with the other.

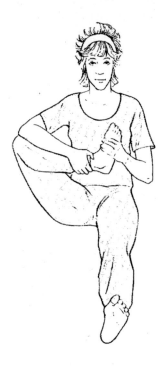

Exercise 3

4. Sit on the floor with your legs stretched out in front of you. Bend the right knee and place the right foot on the left thigh, as near as possible to the top of the leg. If necessary support your body by placing the palms of the hands a little behind and to the outside of the buttocks. Keeping your back straight and your right leg relaxed, hold the position for a minute or two, allowing the knee to come down as close as possible to the floor. Change legs and repeat the exercise.

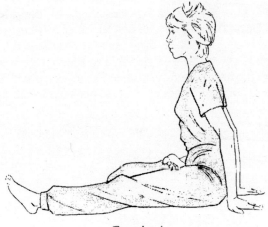

Exercise 4

5. Sit in the same position as in Exercise 4, but instead of
   supporting your body with both hands, support it with the left
   hand only. Place the right hand on the right knee and bounce it
   up and down gently ten times. Change legs and repeat the
   exercise.

Exercise 5

6. Sit on the floor with your legs stretched out. Bend the knees out and bring the soles of the feet together. Without allowing the soles to break contact, draw them towards your body and place the heels as close as possible to the groin. Holding the toes with the hands, gently bounce the knees up and down ten times, bringing the knees as close as possible to the floor.

Exercise 6

7. Sit with your heels as close as possible to your groin as in Exercise 6 but, instead of holding the toes, place the hands on the knees and gently press them as close as possible to the floor. Repeat ten times.

Exercise 7

To sit in the lotus posture

Sit on the floor with your legs stretched out in front of you. Bend the right knee and, taking hold of the right foot with both hands, place it at the top of the left thigh so that the heel presses into the abdomen. Then in the same way place the left foot at the top of the right thigh so that the heel presses into the abdomen. The soles of the feet should be turned up and both knees should touch the ground.

The back should be straight from the base of the spine to the neck, and the abdomen relaxed. The top of the head is held in line with the base of the spine, so that you look straight ahead. The hands can be placed either on the knees or between the heels, one hand over the other.

Half lotus posture

If you find it difficult to sit in the full lotus posture you may like to start with the half lotus. First loosen up with the preparatory exercises described for the full lotus. Then sit on the floor with your legs stretched out in front of you. Bend the left knee and place the left foot beneath the right thigh as close as possible to your buttocks. Then bend the right knee and place the right foot on top of the left thigh as in the full lotus. Both knees should touch the ground and the back should be kept straight, as in the full lotus.

Half lotus posture

Perfect posture (siddhasana)

Sit on the floor with your legs stretched out in front of you. Bend the left knee and, taking hold of the left foot with both hands place the heel against the perineum (between the anus and the genitals). Then bend the right knee and place the heel against the pubic bone. Tuck the toes in between the calf and thigh of the left leg. Keep the spine erect and place the hands as in the lotus position.

Perfect posture

Easy posture

This is a simple cross-legged position in which both feet are kept on the floor. As with all meditation positions, the back should be kept straight but not rigid, and the stomach muscles relaxed. Your weight should be carried by the lower back muscles, and your head, neck and trunk should be in line so that it feels as though your centre of gravity passes from the base of your spine up through the top of your head. You can place your hands on your knees, or in your lap, one on top of the other or lightly clasped.

Easy posture

Sitting on a chair

If you are unable to sit on the floor, sit on a straight-backed chair or, ideally, one of the specially designed posture chairs such as those made by Balans. These backless chairs have slanted seats and knee rests, and encourage upright posture and the correct distribution of weight. Avoid sitting in an armchair or on a soft sofa or bed. They will only encourage slouched posture and drowsiness – not the state of mind meditation seeks to achieve.

If you use a straight-backed chair, sit on the front part of the seat. Placing a small cushion at the back of the chair so that you are sitting on the front edge of it can improve your posture. Place your feet flat on the floor, moving the legs apart slightly so that, when they are relaxed, the lower legs are perpendicular to the floor. Keep your back straight as in the previous positions.

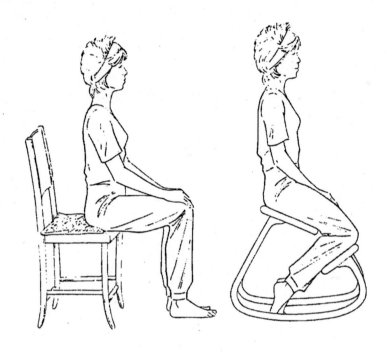

Sitting on a chair

Kneeling posture

Some people find this posture a good alternative to the 'easy' cross-legged posture as it is easier to keep the spine straight in this position. Kneel down with your knees together. Separate the heels and bring the big toes together so that you sit on the insides of the feet. Place the hands on the knees and keep the back straight as in the previous postures.

Kneeling posture

Corpse pose (shavasana)

Lie flat on the floor, preferably with a carpet or folded blanket beneath you, or on a hard mattress. Separate your legs slightly and allow the feet to flop to the sides. Move your arms slightly away from your body and rest the hands on the floor with the palms up. The corpse pose is also ideal for relaxation (see below).

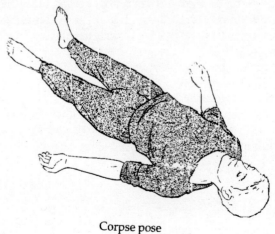

Corpse pose

Relaxing in this way prior to meditation can be very helpful, and some teachers also recommend lying in this pose for a few minutes at the end of meditation.

Eyes

Teachers and traditions differ as to whether the eyes should be kept open or closed during meditation. Some people find it easier to concentrate with the eyes closed, but on the other hand this can encourage drowsiness and daydreaming. Many Zen masters and yoga teachers recommend keeping the eyes half open, and lowering the gaze so that it rests on the floor at a point about a metre away from the body.

Relaxation

Even though meditation itself generally has a relaxing effect, it can be very helpful consciously to relax before meditation if you are at all agitated or tense. The corpse pose, described above, is the ideal posture for complete mental and physical relaxation. Lying flat on your back, go systematically through your body first tightening or flexing the muscles and shaking the joints, then relaxing them. Begin with the toes and feet, then the ankles, calves and so on right up to the top of the head. Don't forget the facial muscles – you cannot possibly be completely relaxed if your forehead is tense or your lips pursed together. Then work through your body again, this time giving each part of the body mental suggestions to relax – 'Toes relax', and so on. When you have worked your way right through your body, scan it for any tension spots and, if necessary, give further mental suggestions to relax. When the entire body is completely relaxed, lie still for a few more minutes, focusing on your breathing. To gain the fullest benefits from the session, lie in this position for a few minutes after you have finished meditating.

If it is inconvenient to lie down, you can try a modified version of this relaxation technique simply giving the various parts of your body mental suggestions to relax, in any of the sitting postures.

Breathing

Another important factor in meditation is the breathing process, and many forms of meditation, examples of which are given in Chapter 4, focus on this. Some complex types of meditation involve certain breathing techniques, but these are beyond the scope of this book and should only be practised under the guidance of a reliable teacher.

Generally speaking, you should not disturb the natural rhythm of the breath. You should breathe through the nose, not the mouth and the breathing process should be natural, not controlled or forced. As meditation deepens and the mind becomes still, the breath will become steadier of its own accord. If, on the other hand, different kinds of breathing patterns – rapid and forceful breathing, or breath retention, for example – occur in a spontaneous way, do not worry. Just allow these changes to take place without interference.

Bellows breathing (bhastrika pranayama)

Providing you have learnt the technique correctly, a few rounds of the yoga technique of *bhastrika* practised before meditation can be a very effective means of stilling the mind. It is best learnt from a teacher because incorrect practice can result in an unpleasant dizzy sensation or even nausea.

Bhastrika is Sanskrit for 'bellows', and just as air is forced into and expelled from a blacksmith's bellows by the rapid and vigorous expansion and contraction of the bellows, in this technique the breath is drawn in and out rapidly by the forceful expansion and contraction of the abdominal muscles. The movement made on exhaling is similar to the movement made when blowing the nose quickly and forcefully.

To practise *bhastrika* you can sit in any of the meditation poses or you can sit on your heels with your knees well apart. Your back must be absolutely straight, and the head and neck in line with the base of the spine. Inhale and exhale rapidly through the nose, with equal emphasis on the inhalation and exhalation, about 10 or 12 times. On the final exhalation, expel all the air from the lungs. Then inhale slowly and deeply, retaining the breath as long as you can without discomfort. Exhale, and take a few normal breaths. This is one round. Repeat two to four times, resting in between each round with a few normal breaths.

Gradually build up the number of breaths in each round to a maximum of 30. If possible lie down in the corpse pose for a few minutes after completing the exercise until the breath becomes quiet and even. Then sit for meditation.

Bhastrika should only be practised on an empty stomach – at least two hours after a light meal and five or six after a heavy one. Wait at least half an hour after finishing before eating. This technique should not be practised by pregnant women or by anyone with high or low blood pressure, or with lung or heart problems.

Attitude

One of the mysteries of meditation is that on the one hand, while effort and self-discipline are necessary, trying too hard and striving for results are counterproductive. Whatever form of meditation you choose – different techniques are described in Chapter 4 – your attention is bound to wander from the meditative focus from time to time, and quite possibly most of the time. Don't bother about the thoughts and images that arise in meditation, and don't try to suppress them or drive them away. Simply notice them without comment, bring your attention back to the focus and continue to meditate. An alternative approach is to follow your thoughts, trying to discover their source – where they come from, and where they go to.

Try to let go of any expectations and keep an open mind. There is no 'right' experience of meditation. Accept your own experience as it is, and don't worry if nothing special seems to be happening.

Coming out of meditation

Never come out of meditation abruptly – you will lose many of the benefits if you do. Remain quietly seated or lying for a few minutes, gently moving or stretching any muscles and joints that need easing, and noting the effect meditation has had. Some teachers recommend lying in the corpse pose (pages 43–44) for a few minutes after meditation.

4

Techniques of meditation

Meditation is like a journey, and techniques of meditation like the transport. Because of people's differing needs and tastes, an enormous number of meditation techniques have evolved, some of which are more direct than others. Most of these methods were originally taught by mystics thousands of years ago and have been handed down from teacher to student for centuries. Some have been adapted over the years according to the time, place and culture within which they have been practised. Others, in their original form, are as appropriate today as they were two thousand years ago. The selection of techniques given in this chapter is by no means comprehensive. The aim is to describe sufficient to enable those with little or no experience of meditation to experiment and find the way that suits them. Selection has also been guided by the need to describe techniques that can be practised without instruction from a teacher.

Deciding which technique to use can be difficult. Remember, however, that techniques are not ends in themselves, but means to achieving a state that lies beyond technique. Some teachers and religious movements make very strong claims for their methods but, while it may be true that some forms of meditation are more universally appealing, or more effective for more people than others, don't be misled into thinking that there is a 'right' way, or even a 'best' way. The best technique for you to start with is the one you feel most drawn to or that feels most natural to you.

You may need to experiment a little to find out which method is best for you, but you will probably be able to rule out some techniques as being unsuitable for you personally without even trying them. Others may seem an obvious choice. For example, if you are an active person and dislike sitting still for long at a time you might try a form of meditation which involves movement, such as Sufi dancing, t'ai chi or hatha yoga. These methods should, however, be learnt from an experienced teacher. Intellectuals are often drawn to the Zen practice of *zazen*, in which no attempt is made to restrict the attention to a particular focus. If you have a devotional nature you might prefer to repeat a name of God as a mantra. Readers with no particular preference are recommended to try the technique of following the breath (method 5, page 50) or the *hamsa* mantra (pages 56–57), another technique which utilizes the breath. Both of these are natural methods which suit most people.

Once you have made an initial choice, give the method a trial run. Sometimes people can tell immediately after one session whether a technique is right for them or not, but unless you have a very strong feeling against it, persevere with the chosen method for a week or two. During the trial period note how you feel before, during and after meditation, and assess the general effects the practice is having on the rest of your life. If, in general, you feel better after meditation than you did before, and if the rest of your life is improved as a result, then continue with the method. If not, experiment with different techniques until you find one you are happy with. Once you have found a method that suits you, you will make faster progress if you persevere with it rather than continue to experiment.

Breath-awareness techniques

To breathe is to live, and in some languages, for example Sanskrit, the word for 'breath' is also the word for 'life' or 'spirit'. The way a person breathes is intimately connected with their state of mind and their general physical and mental condition. For example, when a person is relaxed their breathing is smooth and regular, and fairly slow, but when angry or agitated, it is noisy, irregular and fast. In moments of deep concentration, or when making a great physical effort, it is natural to hold the breath. This connection between the breath and mental and physical states has been recognized in most cultures, many of which have consciously used breath control to induce specific states of mind, as well as to improve health. For example in healthcare breathing exercises are widely used as part of stress management programmes; pregnant women are also taught certain breathing exercises to ease the process of giving birth. Control of the breath is considered so important in yoga that an entire branch of yoga, called *pranayama*, is devoted to it (*prana* means 'breath', 'spirit', 'life force', 'vitality'). The yogic breath-control technique known as *bhastrika* ('bellows' breathing), discussed in Chapter 3, is recommended as an aid to meditation. After practising *bhastrika* the breathing will become calm and quiet, helping to still the mind. This exercise is best learnt from an experienced teacher who has mastered the technique.

Awareness of breathing has been recognized by many schools and traditions of meditation as an effective means of stilling the mind, and many techniques are built around it. The reason that breath-awareness techniques are described first in this chapter is because they are natural techniques which most people feel comfortable with and find effective. Furthermore, although they are practised in some form or other in all the major traditions, most are entirely neutral with respect to religious or philosophical belief.

In the techniques described in this section the breath provides the sole focus of attention. But awareness of the breathing can also be combined with other techniques such as mantra repetition, and in particular the *hamsa* mantra, which, although described at the end of the section on mantras (pages 56–57), is essentially a breath-awareness technique.

Unlike breath-control exercises, in meditation you should breathe naturally, without interfering with the rhythm of the breath. Breath-awareness techniques of meditation simply involve being aware of the breath as it comes in and out. Your breathing will become smoother and more regular of its own accord, and there is no need to control it consciously. You may find that breath retention happens spontaneously, or that your breathing becomes either very slow and shallow, or that the pattern of breathing alters during the meditation in some other way. This is perfectly natural and an indication that meditation is progressing. However if you feel alarmed discontinue the practice until you have a chance to discuss what is happening with an experienced teacher.

How to meditate using breath-awareness techniques

Choose from any of the following methods for focusing attention on the breath. The technique of counting breaths (method 1) can be combined with breath-awareness techniques involving concentration on a particular part of the body such as the abdomen or the tip of the nostrils (methods 2 and 3), or the point in the centre of the eyebrows, the crown of the head or the heart.

1. Sit comfortably in an upright position, either on the floor or on a chair, or lie down. Close your eyes and relax. Breathing naturally, count your breaths on either the exhalation or the inhalation from one to ten, repeating the procedure throughout the meditation.

   When thoughts or feelings arise, as they inevitably will, simply allow them to come and go, keeping your attention focused on counting the breaths. If there are external noises and distractions, just let them be. If your attention wanders and you lose count, gently bring it back to the breathing and start counting from one again.

2. Sit comfortably in an upright position, either on the floor or on a chair, or lie down. Close your eyes and relax. Breathing naturally, focus your attention on the sensation at the tip of your nostrils as the breath flows in and out of the body. Again, observe a passive attitude to the thoughts and feelings that pass through your mind and, if your attention wanders, gently bring it back to the task in hand.

3. Instead of focusing on the tip of the nostrils, as in method 2, concentrate your attention on the movement of the abdomen as you inhale and exhale.

4. Sit comfortably in an upright position, either on the floor or on a chair, or lie down. Close your eyes and relax. Breathing naturally, focus your attention on the spaces between breaths – on the space outside the body where the exhalation ends, and the inner space in the centre of the body where the inhalation ends. At each of these points there is a moment of complete stillness.

   Observe a passive attitude to mental distractions and if your attention wanders, gently bring it back to the breathing. With practice the spaces between breaths will increase, and your mind will become very still.

5. Sit comfortably in an upright position, either on the floor or on a chair, or lie down. Close your eyes and relax. Breathing naturally, follow your breath as it comes in and out. Try to merge your mind with the breath, becoming one with it and flowing with it. Come in with the inhalation and go out with the exhalation, resting momentarily in the spaces between breaths.

Observe a passive attitude to mental distractions and if your attention wanders, gently rejoin it with the breath.

There are many variations on the methods described above, such as counting to five instead of ten, concentrating on the inner space between breaths only, and so on. You can experiment to find out what suits you. You may also like to spend part of your meditation session practising one method, such as counting the breath, and the rest of the session practising another, such as following the breath. However it is best, at least to begin with, to decide exactly which technique or techniques you are going to use before beginning the session and then stick to your plan. Switching from one technique to another during meditation can often be a symptom of feeling unsettled, rather than a sign that the technique you are using is not effective. Then, when you have made an initial choice, give the method a trial run (page 48).

Mantra

The repetition of a mantra is probably the most popular form of meditation and, because of this, more space is devoted to this technique than to others. A mantra is a usually sacred sound which can be chanted or repeated silently as a form of meditation. The basis of mantra is sound, and the science of mantra is based on the power of sound to affect people and produce different states in them.

Nearly all religious and mystical traditions recognize the creative power of sound and nearly all use it in various forms, such as hymns, plainsong, chants and prayers, to uplift and purify the soul, and to glorify God. The gospel of St John opens with the verse 'In the beginning was the Word, and the Word was with God, and the Word was God'. A strikingly similar passage from the Vedic scriptures of India translates: 'In the beginning was Prajapati (the Lord of all creatures) with whom was the Word, and the Word is the supreme Brahman.' It is not only religious traditions that hold that the creation of the universe began with sound. Modern scientists holding the big bang theory – the theory that the universe originated in the explosion of a single mass of material – hold fundamentally the same view.

Fascinating as the theory of mantra is, it is not necessary to turn either to scriptural authority or to modern science to under-stand just how powerful sound can be. Someone only has to call you by an abusive name for your blood to boil and your whole mood change. An unpleasant noise like squeaky chalk can make your flesh crawl. This being so, it seems reasonable to suppose that a pure sound or word is likely to have a more beneficial effect than a mundane one. However people who find this method of meditation effective, but who wish to avoid any suggestion of cultishness or religion, often prefer to repeat a meaningless phrase. There is plenty of experimental evidence to indicate that repetition of any sound has a relaxing effect, which can only be beneficial, but whether it has the same profound effect as a spiritual mantra is open to doubt.

The science of sound

Sound is actually a form of energy produced by a vibrating object or system and transmitted by waves. Each object or system has its own natural frequency of vibration and, depending upon this frequency, a particular wavelength is produced when it vibrates. The human ear is receptive to waves within a certain frequency band, and the different frequencies within this band are inter-preted by the brain as different sounds. Frequencies below the range of human hearing are called infrasonic, frequencies above ultrasonic. Although it is only through the ear that sound is actually 'heard', sound waves of all frequencies are received by the whole body and absorbed by it, and there are deaf musicians who perform by feeling sound through their skin. Sound has a powerful effect on the body, some sounds being highly therapeu-tic, others the reverse, and this principle is now being used by some therapists.

Connected to the phenomena of sound and vibration is that of resonance, whereby a strong vibration can be set up in one system by means of another vibrating at the same frequency. For example, if you strike one tuning fork and hold another of the same frequency near it, it will resonate – in other words sympathetically produce the same note without actually being struck itself. It is to avoid setting up damaging resonance that soldiers break step over a bridge. A basic understanding of sound, vibration and resonance helps to an understanding of the theory behind mantra.

The science of mantra

As explained in Chapter 2, modern physics views mass as nothing but a form of energy. Furthermore, it holds that mind and matter are connected forms of the same pulsating energy. The ancient science of mantra is in line with this view, but goes a step further, analysing this energy in terms of sounds, however subtle, of different vibratory levels. Sound then, as it is referred to in this science, is not just the form of sound that we experience at an everyday level. Rather it exists and can be experienced at all levels of subtlety. According to some traditions, for example the system of yoga, different sounds resonate with different energy centres in the body, and these sounds are combined in particular ways to form a mantra. Mantra is said to be the sound form of God, and different mantras represent different forms or aspects of God. Thus to the power of sound is added the power of meaning. None of the great traditional mantras are just arbitrary collections of sound – they are carefully constructed to purify the body and transform consciousness.

The mantra om (aum)

Symbol for the mantra *om*

The Sanskrit word *om* (pronounced 'home' without the 'h') is the supreme Hindu mantra and is said to be the primordial sound, the word from which the entire universe arises. *Om* appears both as a monosyllable, in which form it is often combined with other sounds or words to form multisyllabic mantras, such as *om mani padme hum* or *om namah shivaya*, and as the three sounds *a* (as in 'father'), *u* (as in 'good'), *m*, of which it consists. Great spiritual power is attributed both to the whole word and to the three sounds, and this mantra is said to have the highest value as an object of meditation. The graphic representation of this mantra can also be used in visual meditation.

In its original sense, *om* can be compared with the word 'Amen'. It is placed at the beginning and end of Hindu prayers and is sometimes translated as 'verily' or 'so be it'. Later it was used as the mystic name for the Hindu triad, representing the union of the three gods *a* (Vishnu), *u* (Shiva) and *m* (Brahma). (Although various deities are associated with Hinduism, these deities are regarded as different aspects of the one supreme God or reality.)

To test for yourself the way different sounds vibrate in different parts of the body, repeat *a-u-m* (*aah-ooh-mm*) aloud, slowly and resonantly, several times over. Allow one beat for each letter, and allow an extra beat after sounding the final *m* before repeating the mantra again. Notice how the sound ascends from the base of the throat to the mouth, and how at the same time resonance is set up in the navel travelling up through the body to the top of the head. The sound *a* vibrates in the navel, *u* in the heart. The sound *m* vibrates first in the mouth, then the vibration continues up between the eyebrows to the crown of the head.

In meditation the mantra is usually repeated silently. However, many teachers believe that repeating mantras aloud, especially as a group activity, is an aid to meditation as well as having a profound healing effect.

Choosing a mantra

If you feel comfortable with their sacred or mystical associations, try meditating with the mantra *om* (*aum*) or with one of the following:

- *om namah shivaya*, a traditional and well-known Indian mantra meaning literally 'I bow to Shiva', or loosely 'I honour my own inner self' (Shiva being the self of all)
- *om mani padme hum*, literally 'the jewel in the lotus' another traditional and famous mantra, much used by Tibetan Buddhists
- *la ilaha illa'llah,* a line from the Koran used as a mantra in the Sufic tradition, and meaning 'There is no God but Allah'
- *kyrie eleison,* a Greek phrase used in the Christian tradition, meaning 'Lord have mercy'

- *maranatha*, Aramaic for 'Come, Lord', used by Christians
- *abba*, Aramaic for 'Father', used by Jesuits
- *hallelujah* or *alleluia*, Hebrew for 'praise the Lord'
- *ANoKhY*, 'I am', used in the Jewish tradition

If you want to use a spiritual mantra, but do not feel comfortable with any of the above, use any name of God or inspiring phrase that is not too long from a sacred text. Some Christians use the following as mantras:

'Be still and know that I am God'

'Lord Jesus Christ, son of God, have mercy upon me'
This prayer can also be used in a shorter form:
'Lord Jesus Christ' – on the inhalation
'Have mercy upon me' – on the exhalation

If you prefer to use a neutral or meaningless mantra, choose any sound or word that appeals to you, the shorter the better. Otherwise, if you feel you would do better with a mantra which has positive associations, without having religious or mystical overtones, you could try using phrases and words such as 'Be here now', 'love', 'peace' or 'harmony'. Some people successfully use their own name as a mantra.

Once you have settled on a mantra you feel good with, stick to it. When the same mantra is repeated over and over again it becomes more effective, as well as becoming a tool you can use at odd moments in your everyday life to calm you down or focus your attention when life gets hectic or trying.

How to meditate with a mantra

Sit comfortably in an upright position, either on the floor or on a chair, or lie down. Close your eyes and relax. Breathing naturally, repeat your chosen mantra silently at a normal speaking rate. If you wish, you can repeat the mantra in rhythm with your breathing, once or twice on the inhalation, once or twice on the exhalation. Immerse yourself in the mantra and become absorbed in it. Lose yourself in meditation. If you are using a spiritual mantra, repeat it with the awareness that the goal of the mantra is your own inner self – that you, the mantra and the goal of the mantra are all one.

Once your mind has become still it is unnecessary to carry on repeating the mantra. Don't worry if thoughts and images pass through your mind. Allow them to come and go, keeping your attention focused on the mantra. If you find your attention wandering, gently bring it back to repetition of the mantra.

The *hamsa* (*so'ham*) technique

The *hamsa* technique, expounded in an ancient Sanskrit text on yoga called the *Vijñānabhairava*, is a simple and natural technique of watching the breath coming in and going out. As the breath comes in it is said to make the sound *ha*, as it goes out the sound *sah*. At the junction between the *ha* and the *sah* the *m* occurs automatically. Thus *hamsa* is continuously repeated by every living being, whether they are aware of it or not, and for this reason it is referred to as a mantra. It is also called the natural mantra as it is repeated spontaneously, without any effort, rather than being recited mentally or aloud.

The meaning of the mantra is 'I am that' (*aham* 'I am', *sah* 'that'), indicating the identity of the individual self with the universal self. When *hamsa* is consciously and repeatedly contemplated, it becomes *so'ham*, 'that am I'. This is because, according to Sanskrit rules of grammar, *sah* followed by *aham* forms the combination *so'ham*. *Hamsa* and *so'ham* are thus the same mantra and have the same meaning. Reversing the syllables simply shifts the emphasis from individual awareness to universal awareness.

How to meditate using the hamsa (so'ham) *technique*

Sit comfortably in a quiet place with your eyes half or fully closed, as described in Chapter 3. Breathing naturally, become aware of the sound of the breath as you inhale and exhale, *ha* on the inhalation, *sah* (or *so*) on the exhalation. Focus your attention on the spaces between each breath – on the inner space between the *ha* and *sah* where the sound *m* is produced, and the outer space where *sah* dissolves, before *ha* arises.

If thoughts and images pass through your mind, allow them to come and go, keeping your attention focused on your breathing. If your attention wanders, gently bring it back to the breath. With practice you will find that the space between the breaths increases, and the mind becomes very still. However, it is important that you allow this process to happen of its own accord, without interfering with the natural rhythm of your breathing.

Visual meditation

Pictorial and symbolical images are used in almost all mystical and religious traditions to inspire and evoke greater spiritual awareness and this has resulted, in some traditions, in exquisite works of art. In the Eastern Orthodox Church, for example, icons – typically paintings on small wooden panels of Christ, the Virgin Mary or a Saint – have long been used as an aid to devotional practices. Mystical diagrams are much used as an aid to meditation in the East, most particularly in certain Buddhist and Hindu traditions. Such diagrams have probably reached their fullest expression and greatest complexity in the glorious *mandalas* of tantric yoga, with their rich colours, imagery and symbolism. These diagrams, which are discussed in more detail below, form the basis of meditation for the tantric student, and are specifically designed to turn the attention within and enhance spiritual development.

Images of such complexity are not, however, necessary and newcomers are recommended to begin the practice of visual meditation by gazing at, and subsequently visualizing, a simple neutral object. More complicated images can gradually be attempted as skill in visualization develops. A lighted candle in a darkened room is one of the easiest ways to start. A flame naturally focuses the attention, just as a fireplace provides a natural focal point in a room, and is an easy image to maintain mentally. The practice of visual meditation begins with gazing at the chosen object or symbol. The eyes are then closed and the object is visualized internally, the latter being the more subtle practice. In the early stages of meditation it can be quite difficult to hold a precise mental picture, and the meditator generally spends much of the time with his or her eyes open, looking at the physical object or image. With practice it becomes easier to hold a mental image steadily, and eventually the physical object can be dispensed with entirely.

The kind of meditation that is the subject of this section should not be confused with the visualization that is often used in therapeutic contexts or as an aid to self-healing, self-improvement and so on. This latter sort of visualization usually relies on some form of guided fantasy designed to give the visualizer or the therapist insight into character or personal problems, or it may consist of a series of positive affirmations, and so on. Here a deliberate thought process is taking place, whereas in the kind of meditation dealt with in this book the objective is to still the mind and empty it of thought, adopting whatever techniques are conducive to this thought-free state. The purpose of gazing at and visualizing an object is to focus the attention. The aim is to be aware of the object without thinking creatively or rationally about it, or free-associating. The meditator experiences rather than thinks about the object, absorbing him- or herself in it and uniting with it.

Another form of visualization used in some meditation systems involves the creation of intricate mental constructs entirely from the imagination. This sort of meditation is taken to its extreme limits in the tantric mysticism of Tibet, in which adepts mentally create deities with which they then identify, taking on the qualities of the beings so created. Visualizations of this kind are beyond the scope of this book and should not be attempted except under the guidance of a reliable teacher.

Choosing a visual object or image

As already mentioned, a lighted candle or other light source against a dark background provides an ideal focus of attention for beginners, but any simple object or image can be used – preferably one which is attractive and has neutral associations. Natural objects are a popular choice, for example a flower, a blade of grass or a stone. Geometrical shapes, such as a sphere, or colours can also be used to great effect.

The *kasina* meditations described in a fourth-century Buddhist text called the *Visuddhimagga* list ten different *kasinas* or subjects for visual meditation. These comprise the four elements: earth, air, fire and water; the four colours: blue, yellow, red and white; and light and space. To meditate on one of the four elements, the meditator gazes at an appropriate object, such as a dish filled with earth, something like the branches of a tree, moving in the wind, a flame or a bowl of water. For meditation on one of the colours, the meditator gazes at any object of the appropriate colour. This may simply be a sheet of paper or a disc painted in the chosen colour, or it could be a flower of a particular colour, a leaf, a cushion and so on. Meditation on light can be practised by looking at a patch of light cast by a spotlight, the reflection of light on water, or rays of light filtering through foliage. An empty container or the space between objects could serve as the focus of attention for meditation on space.

Mystic and religious symbols

Mystical and religious traditions provide a wealth of material that can be used as sources for visual meditation. The best known religious symbol in the Western world is the Cross, the emblem of Christianity. Another symbol familiar to many is the Buddhist Wheel of Life or Becoming, which symbolizes on one level the cycle of existence and the illusory nature of the world as perceived by the senses, and on another level can be seen as a map of the human mind.

Yet another is the Chinese *yin-yang* symbol, which illustrates the creation of the universe – the world of forms and objects – from *t'ai chi*, the cosmic energy or ultimate reality, which is pure, undifferentiated and formless. The circle, representing t'ai chi, is divided into *yin* (the dark area) and *yang* (the light area). *Yin* and *yang* represent the negative and positive poles of t'ai chi and are associated with all the pairs of opposites – feminine and masculine, night and day, passive and active, moon and sun, and so on. Each, however, contains within itself the seed of the other, symbolized by the tiny circles in the diagram.

A symbol from the Jewish mystical tradition is the Tree of Life, a diagram representing the ten divine energies, or Sefirot, which

Yin-yang symbol

create and sustain the physical universe. These energies are also said to correspond to locations in the human body, like the chakras (see pages 64–66) in the system of yoga.

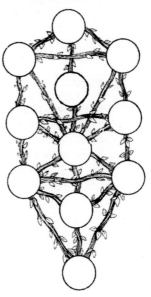

Tree of Life

Serpent

Other well-known symbols are the cosmic egg – the seed of life and symbol of creation – and the serpent, a more esoteric symbol which in Indian philosophy represents the *kundalini*, the latent spiritual energy within all beings.

It would be impossible to list all the symbols that could be used, but those attracted to this form of meditation will be able to find one which appeals to them or which represents their own particular religious or philosophical bias. Mythology is also a rich source for such symbolism and imagery.

Another approach to visual meditation involves gazing at the written form of sacred words and sounds. The art of calligraphy is considered an act of contemplation in itself in some traditions, and letters symbolizing mantras or sacred sounds, such as *om* (illustrated on page 53) or 'Amen', can be used as a focus for visual meditation, especially in combination with mental repetition of the sounds represented (see Mantras on pages 51–56).

Mandalas and yantras

Mandala, a Sanskrit word meaning 'circle' and referring to anything round, is the name given to certain kinds of diagrams designed specifically for meditation. These diagrams are based on a number of concentric circles and squares, and often include concentric or interlocking triangles. The central core is of particular significance, symbolizing on the one hand the inner self and on the other cosmic energy or divine consciousness. The outer circles and rings of lotus petals represent the universe, the

Outline of a mandala

unfolding of creation. Thus the mandala represents the micro-
cosm and the macrocosm, the personal and the transpersonal.
Figures of Buddhas, Bodhisattvas and various deities are sometimes contained within the design, and the diagrams are usually
richly coloured, the colours being chosen for their effect on the
psyche. Mandalas may be very elaborate, their entire surface
being covered with intricate designs having particular symbolic
meaning, or they may be very simple. Either way the basic
principle they exemplify is the same – the fundamental unity of
all things.

These diagrams originated in India and there are both Hindu
and Buddhist mandalas, the best known of which is the Wheel of
Life, mentioned above. But the form of the circle is universal and
it appears widely in different cultures as a spiritual or religious
symbol, as for example the yin-yang symbol (see page 59). The
circle naturally symbolizes the universe, the cycle of life, the
cyclic pattern of the seasons, the psyche, and so on. The great
analytic psychologist Carl Jung discovered that some of his
patients who had never seen a mandala or the yin-yang symbol
nevertheless sometimes saw them in dreams or through intro-
spection. From this he concluded that such symbols were part of
the collective unconsciousness and represented the psyche.

Similar to a mandala is a *yantra*, a mystical diagram supposed
to possess occult powers. The literal meaning of this Sanskrit
term is 'instrument', and these diagrams, which are associated
with the mystical side of Hinduism and in particular with tantric
yoga, are instruments for attaining divine consciousness. The
main difference between a mandala and a yantra is that a yantra
is a graphic representation of a specific aspect of the divine, as

Wheel picture of Brother Klaus, a fifteenth-century Christian mystic

Om yantra, representing the energy pattern of the mantra *om (aum)*

Kali yantra, representing the subtle form of the goddess Kali

The Sanskrit symbol for *krim*, the seed mantra or sound form of the goddess Kali

exemplified by a particular deity, while a mandala has more general significance. A yantra is the visual equivalent of a mantra. If the latter is viewed as the sound form of God, with different mantras representing different aspects of God or divine consciousness, then the former is the diagrammatic representation of this.

The best known and most important yantra is the Shri yantra shown below. As with a mandala, the most important part of the yantra is the central point or *bindu*, which is usually coloured white. This spot represents pure undifferentiated consciousness or energy, the seed of creation, the essence of being. It is to this point of consciousness that the meditator is drawn, and it is here that the meditator discovers their link with the macrocosm. The sound form of the bindu is the 'm' which is added to all *bija*, or seed, mantras. All bija mantras must end with this sound because it is at this point that the meditator experiences his or her identity with universal consciousness. The series of interwoven triangles in the Shri yantra represents the evolutionary process, the outer circles and rings of lotus petals the unfolded reality of the physical world. The bija mantra corresponding to a yantra may be repeated mentally while meditating on the yantra.

The Shri yantra

Chakras

An esoteric practice in tantric and kundalini yoga involves meditating in turn on each of the six main *chakras* (energy centres) spaced along the *sushumna* (central canal) in the subtle body.

The *sahasrara*, or 1000 petalled lotus, is situated at the top of the head. This centre has no seed mantra. It is the centre where all vibrations have their source and finally merge.

The *ajna* chakra is situated in the subtle body between the eyebrows. The seed mantra of this chakra is *om* (the most important *bija*, the primal cosmic vibration)

The *vishuddha* chakra is situated in the subtle body at the throat. The seed mantra of this chakra is *ham* (*bija* of ether)

The *anahata* chakra is situated in the subtle body at the heart. The seed mantra of this chakra is *yam* (*bija* of air)

The *manipura* chakra is situated in the subtle body at the navel. The seed mantra of this chakra is *ram* (*bija* of fire)

The *svadhishtana* chakra is situated in the subtle body below the navel. The seed mantra of this chakra is *vam* (*bija* of water)

The *muladhara* chakra is situated in the subtle body at the base of the spine. The seed mantra of this chakra is *lam* (*bija* of earth)

The kundalini, or serpent power (see Kundalini Yoga pages 87–88), is said to be aroused through meditation on the *muladhara*, the lowest chakra, which is situated in the subtle (psychic) body at a point corresponding to the base of the spine. By meditating successively on each of the succeeding chakras the kundalini progressively unfolds until it ultimately enters the *sahasrara*. This is the highest centre, located at a point in the subtle body corresponding to the crown of the head, or just above the head. It is here that the individual's consciousness is said to merge with universal consciousness, and the seeker experiences mystical union.

The chakras are also called lotuses, and each has a specific number of 'petals' formed by the conjunction of *nadis*, or subtle channels, at each centre. The *muladhara* has 4, the *svadhishtana* 6, the *manipura* 10, the *anahata* 12, the *vishuddha* 16 and the *ajna* 2. On every petal is one of the 50 letters of the Sanskrit alphabet. These 50 letters are reproduced 20 times in the *sahasrara*, which is also known as the 1000-petalled lotus. In addition to these letters each chakra, with the exception of the sahasrara, has a *bija* (seed) mantra at its centre. The bija mantra represents the essential vibration or quality of the chakra and is often repeated mentally while the chakra is visualized.

How to practise visual meditation

Sit comfortably in an upright position, either on the floor or on a chair, or lie down. Close your eyes and relax. The object, symbol or meditative diagram which you have chosen as a focus for meditation should be about a metre or two away from you and roughly level with your eyes. (In the case of a mandala or yantra, the central point should be level with the eyes.) Focus your attention on the object, gazing at it in a relaxed way. Immerse yourself in the object, allowing yourself to become absorbed in it rather than actively thinking about it. After a few minutes close your eyes and visualize the object internally for as long as you can. Repeat the process, alternately opening and closing the eyes as necessary. With practice the mental image seen with the eyes closed will become clearer and more detailed.

Don't worry if thoughts and other images pass through your mind. Allow them to come and go, keeping your attention focused on the object or mental image. If you find your attention wandering, simply bring it back gently to the focal object.

Centring techniques from the *Vijñānabhairava*

The meditations described below are all adapted from an ancient book on yoga called the *Vijñānabhairava*, which described 112 *dharanas* or centring techniques by which the highest state, divine consciousness (the literal meaning of *vijñānabhairava*), can be attained. Although the *Vijñānabhairava* is a book of practical techniques, and not a philosophical book, the mystical practices included arise within the context of a particular metaphysical tradition – that of Kashmir Shaivism.

The book takes the form of a dialogue between Shiva and his consort, the Devi. The Devi, who is already enlightened, questions Shiva about spiritual truths so that other human beings will hear the answers and be able to understand them. Shiva answers that the true nature of the supreme is beyond all form and duality. However he does not reject the world of form, explaining that in fact it is only through the world of forms, and within our ordinary experience, that the supreme state can be attained. The Devi then enquires how this state can be realized, and Shiva replies by suggesting 112 dharanas. Some of these are for formal meditation, for example the *hamsa* technique described on page 00. Some, unlike the other kinds of meditation described in this book, are intended to be used in the course of everyday life, so that common experiences such as the savouring of delicious food or the moment of reunion with a loved one can become a source of illumination. The true practice of such dharanas occurs when you turn your attention away from, for example, the pleasurable taste you experience when eating delicious food, and instead follow that sensation back to its source – the inner self.

1. Sit on a soft seat or bed and contemplate the body as being unsupported and weightless (adapted from dharana 59).
2. Contemplate the skin covering your body as being an empty shell (adapted from dharana 25).
3. Focus on the *sushumna*, the central channel in the subtle body corresponding to the spinal column, and meditate on its inner vacuity (adapted from dharana 12).
4. Concentrate on the idea that the universe is totally void, and let your mind become absorbed in this emptiness (adapted from dharana 35).
5. Contemplate the entire universe, including your own body, as being filled with bliss (adapted from dharana 42).

6. Contemplate the idea that you are omniscient, omnipotent and omnipresent (adapted from dharana 85).
   Note This dharana expresses three ideas which can be taken separately as three different meditations, i.e. 'I am all-knowing', 'I am all-powerful' and 'I am everywhere at all times'.
7. Sitting cross-legged, sway gently from side to side or in a circular movement (adapted from dharana 60).
8. Concentrate on the intermediate state between sleep and waking, when you are on the point of falling asleep. This is called the *turiya* or transcendental state of consciousness (adapted from dharana 52).

The next four dharanas are examples of how sensuous pleasures can become means of yoga. In each of these dharanas the emphasis is on contemplation of the source of pleasure rather than on the sensuous objects or activities in themselves.

9. Meditate on the delight of remembering intense sexual pleasure (adapted from dharana 47).
   Note Since one can experience this delight in the absence of a partner simply through memory, then it must come from within.
10. On any occasion of great happiness, such as seeing a long-absent friend or relative, contemplate the delight itself and become absorbed in it (adapted from dharana 48).
11. When eating or drinking, savour the pleasure arising from the food or drink and becoming absorbed in it (adapted from dharana 49).
12. Absorb yourself completely in the joy of music or song, or other objects (adapted from dharana 50).
    Note The examples of sensuous pleasure given in the previous three dharanas concerned physical pleasures, whereas the main example given in this dharana is of aesthetic pleasure. According to the philosophy of Kashmir Shaivism, one can only experience intense aesthetic pleasure when the mind is completely withdrawn from the external world and rests in the inner self. For this reason aesthetic pleasure is considered a greater source for the experience of divine consciousness.

Zazen

Zazen or 'sitting meditation' is a practice associated with the Zen Buddhist tradition (both Soto and Rinzai Zen). The different schools of Zen have developed different ways of dealing with the mind in meditation, but fundamentally the practice involves, as its name suggests, simply sitting still for a period of time in a state of quiet awareness. Unlike the varieties of meditation discussed so far in this chapter, zazen does not normally involve restricting the attention by focusing on a particular object of meditation such as the breath, a mantra or a mystical diagram (although Zen students are sometimes instructed to begin the practice of meditation by counting breaths from one to ten, see page 50). Zazen is an opening out of attention, so that the meditator is conscious of whatever is happening both externally in their surroundings and internally, in the form of thoughts and fantasies passing through the mind. No deliberate attempt is made either to shut out or to cultivate thoughts, which are simply allowed to come and go without interference or judgement. It is important that the meditator should remain attentive and alert, and Zen students usually keep their eyes partially open during meditation to discourage drowsiness and withdrawal from the world.

How to practise zazen

Most Zen masters place great importance on posture during meditation, especially the correct position of the back. Ideally you should sit on the front edge of a fairly flat, firm cushion in the lotus posture, but if this is uncomfortable then you can sit on a chair or in any of the sitting postures described in Chapter 3. Place your hands on your lap, left over right or lightly clasped, and keep your eyes open with the gaze lowered so that it falls at a point on the floor about a metre away from you. Breathe naturally, through the nose, and just continue to sit, aware of whatever is happening in the present moment.

Thoughts and impressions are bound to arise. Don't judge them, get caught up in them or try to push them away. Just allow them to come and go without bothering about them. Don't try to shut out any sounds, smells or other sense stimuli in your surroundings. Simply be aware of them as pure sounds, smells, and so on, without mentally commenting on what they are or might be due to. There should be no striving, no sense of purpose.

When the meditation period is over, move your body around gently in circles and then stretch out your limbs to ease any stiffness caused by sitting still before getting up.

The koan

Another form of training used in Zen Buddhism is the study of *koans*, a method unique to Zen which is designed to bring about in the student a direct, intuitive experience of absolute reality. Essential to this practice is the relationship between teacher and student, but a brief description of the system is included in this book as it is an important technique which readers interested in joining a Zen meditation group will certainly come across.

The system of koans arose from the questions students asked the early Zen masters. The masters took advantage of the opportunities thus presented to cut through conceptual thinking and awaken deeper understanding in the students. Later the words of these early masters were used in a systematized form, both as a teaching device and as a means of judging a student's degree of attainment or realization, and referred to as koans. The study of koans is associated mainly with Rinzai Zen, in which it is considered of equal importance to the practice of zazen. Koans also have a place in Soto Zen, but the use of koans is secondary in this school and the method of using them different.

In its modern form, the koan system is largely the work of the eighteenth-century Rinzai master Hakuin. Hakuin reformed and revitalized Zen, systematizing the koans and their methods of use as well as creating many new ones, such as the famous 'sound of one hand'. In Rinzai Zen a student is not given a koan until he or she has first practised zazen and acquired some competence. When he or she is sufficiently prepared by practice of zazen, the master will select a koan which is then worked on during zazen. (Generally speaking, in Soto Zen the koan is studied only outside the practice of zazen.)

There are five graduated groups of koan in the Rinzai school, the first group being for beginners, and intended to give the student a glimpse of ultimate reality. Hakuin's 'sound of one hand' is a typical first koan, as is asking the student to discover their 'original face' – or original nature – as it is before they were born. Another is *wu* (Japanese *mu*) – the famous 'No!' of Joshu, a renowned Chinese Zen master, to the question 'Does a dog have the Buddha nature?'

The student concentrates on the koan he or she has been given, often for weeks or months on end. The approach to koan is entirely non-intellectual. The student tries to become one with the koan, to lose him- or herself in it, until the koan fills the whole of their consciousness and the principle it embodies is understood. The teacher will know from the answer given whether or not the student has understood the koan, and if they have not, they must continue working on it. The answers to koans are not usually verbal, for example the reply to 'the bell in the distant temple' could quite well be expressed by making a 'bong' sound, similar to that made by the bell. When the koan has been solved, and the teacher has acknowledged the answer, another koan will be given. The ultimate 'goal' of this kind of Zen training is *satori*, or 'awakening'.

Thus the study of the koan is a method of teaching which, although relying on the relationship between teacher and student, does not involve creeds, doctrines or discussion, and can be practised both during meditation and in the course of normal daily activities.

5

Teachers and traditions

The real guru is he who kills the idol you have made of him.

Rumi

This chapter is primarily aimed at those who may wish to use meditation as part of a spiritual path. If you are using meditation to improve your physical and mental health, you may find it helpful to go to someone who can teach an effective and practical meditation technique. However, if you are looking for a spiritual guide, you will be investing a great deal of yourself in your teacher, and you will want someone with integrity, experience and maturity. There are many different notions of what a spiritual teacher, or guru, is. One view of the spiritual master is that he or she is somehow all-knowing and perfect. However, in the West there is no precedent for this tradition, and it is not reasonable for teachers to expect their students to adopt a position of unquestioning acceptance and obedience. Teachers who behave in this way invariably set themselves up for a fall, and the subsequent sense of disillusion among their students is strong. The truth is that teachers are as human as anybody else, and we should not have unreasonable expectations of them. Once we take this practical stance towards teachers, we can feel more confident about finding what we are looking for. The right teacher will be somebody with whom you feel an affinity, and whom you respect. A good teacher is invaluable and will give you confidence, reassurance and encouragement.

Another reason for working with a teacher is that, in any tradition, teachings tend to be interpreted differently by each successive generation. Additions to a particular technique often detract from its effectiveness, and learning meditation under an experienced teacher usually ensures that the technique is not adulterated by the additions of inexperienced students.

An additional advantage lies simply in having someone there to answer the questions which inevitably arise as you progress.

Because meditation is a personal experience which varies from individual to individual, each person's experience remains unique, and no one book or set of teachings, however comprehensive, can hope to answer all the questions likely to arise. However, a good teacher will be well aware of the students' differing needs and circumstances, and will give them individual guidance according to their particular personality and stage of development. The company and support of other meditators working with the same teacher can also be helpful. It is sometimes very reassuring to discover that others encounter similar problems – whether of keeping the mind still, of aching knees, or simply of finding the time to meditate each day.

Finding the right teacher

In the initial stages of practice, you will probably benefit from working with anyone who has some experience of meditation. The more your practice develops, however, the more demanding it can become, and the more selective you need to be. Although you will probably learn from a number of different people if you become seriously interested in meditation, you will learn very little if you are constantly chopping and changing teachers. Therefore you should be initially cautious in choosing a teacher, and think carefully before changing to someone else. Real progress in meditation takes time and commitment, which means working with the same method and the same teacher over an extended period of time.

However, at a time when people are sceptical of the claims of many teachers, and suspicious of their motives, and when the word 'guru' is synonymous in many minds with fraud, the task of identifying a valid teacher, let alone the right teacher for yourself, can be daunting. One of the objects of this chapter is to provide some basic guidelines for assessing and selecting a teacher. These are particularly relevant if you are practising meditation as a spiritual discipline.

What are the teacher's qualifications?

The main qualification of a teacher is experience in meditation, skill in the technique being taught and knowledge about the process of meditation. Many people also feel that a *spiritual* teacher should have studied under a teacher and should acknowledge the tradition from which they inherited their own knowledge. The value of tradition – the successive handing down of knowledge from teacher to student over generations – is of immense importance. Not only does this ensure that the purity of the teaching is not lost, it also means that the authority of the teaching is derived from a lineage, not from just one individual.

What kind of a person is the teacher?

It is not essential that you form a great personal attachment to your teacher, although it does of course help if you find their personality congenial. More important than this is whether they practise what they preach, and whether they are good examples of their teachings. Just as you would think twice about going to a neurotic psychotherapist, you should keep away from a teacher whose character or lifestyle does not set a good example. Before accepting a teacher, try to find out a bit about them. Are they responsible, trustworthy, and stable individuals? Do they relate well with other people – not just with their students, but with their families and outsiders? How well do they cope with difficult situations? Are they generally cheerful or do they tend to be nervous or depressed? What aspects of themselves do they most cultivate? Are they simply highly charismatic characters who have a way with words but no substance to their teachings? No matter how strong a claim a teacher may make to be the inheritor of an ancient lineage, and guardian of the truth, if the score on a personal level is not good, look elsewhere.

What effect are the teachings having on you?

The best test of whether or not you are working with the right teacher is the effect that following their teachings has upon you. Initial selection of a teacher or system is often based on gut feeling. This can be a very reliable guide, but should always be balanced with an intelligent and objective assessment. If a teacher and a tradition he or she represents 'feel' right to you, then go ahead and give them a fair trial. If, over the course of a few months, you find you are in sympathy with the teachings and benefiting from the techniques you are given, as well as having personal respect for the teacher, then you may be fairly confident that you have found what you are looking for.

However, you should always take into account the tradition which a teacher represents before making any commitment. In the early stages of involvement the philosophical or religious beliefs, if any, underlying the teachings may seem relatively unimportant. Later on, they can become an issue. However, if the essential teachings appeal to you, do not be put off by superficialities.

Other students

It is also a good idea to observe the other students when choosing a teacher. More important than their personalities is the effect that following the teachings has had on them – whether as a result they are stronger, more independent, more aware and more honest people than before, whether the quality of their lives has improved. Observe also the interaction between the teacher and his or her students. If the teacher demands uncritical acceptance and obedience, you should be very cautious. Teachers should help to increase the strength and self-reliance of their followers, not make them more dependent.

Bear in mind, however, that it is very easy to be put off by the behaviour and attitudes of one or two individuals in a group, who may not even be practising the teachings seriously, and allow this to interfere with your assessment of the teacher's real worth. People are drawn to a teacher or group for many different reasons and no reputable teacher will turn away students on the grounds of their looks, smell, personality, or intelligence! Because one may rightly have exacting standards in one's search for a teacher, this can easily spill over into having unrealistic expectations of their students. This said, though, you are unlikely to make much progress surrounded by a group of people who consistently irritate you.

Teachers to avoid

Knowing what to avoid when looking for a teacher is not as straightforward a matter as it might at first seem. Extortionate fees, excessive secrecy, inefficient organization and extravagant claims are a few indications that are too obvious to need underlining. There are one or two rules of thumb, however, which, while not infallible, can be a useful guide.

1. A teacher who claims to be enlightened or self-realized, yet fails to acknowledge any tradition or teacher, is probably best avoided. In particular, a teacher who appears to encourage a personality cult should be regarded with caution.
2. Another, and more subjective, piece of advice is not to be misled by spectacular initial experiences into automatically accepting a teacher without longer acquaintance. The greatest benefits of meditation are long-term, and do not lie in sensational experiences. In fact, good teachers will actively discourage their students from paying too much attention to what happens during meditation. The fact that you may have visions or feelings of great ecstasy during meditation does not necessarily mean that your teacher is the next messiah! Such experiences can happen through the application of a number of fairly simple techniques. Any teacher who encourages students to identify with these to the exclusion of longer-term benefits should be viewed with caution.
3. A third kind of teacher to be wary of is one who uses a jumble of different techniques from diverse sources. A person who teaches yoga and Sufi dancing in addition to primal therapy and psychosynthesis is unlikely to have mastered any one of these techniques fully. While the experiences round such a figure may well be exciting, they are unlikely to lead to substantial, long-term benefits. A teacher who imparts one mantra and says very little is likely to offer much more.
4. Any teacher who demands unquestioning obedience, or encourages students to become dependent on them, is best avoided. Real teachers, like good parents, want their students to be independent and autonomous, taking responsibility for their own lives and making their own decisions. If you find people constantly asking their teacher where they should live and what they should call their cat, be circumspect.

To sum up, finding the right teacher is very much a matter of not allowing yourself to be put off by superficial details but at the same time not being naive. Do not immediately assume the worst if the organization appears to be comfortably off, unless you find that the less wealthy are discouraged from being involved. However, secrecy about how the organization is run, or a lack of openness about the past history of the group may be signs that all is not well. Do not be misled, by your own preconceptions as to how a teacher should be and what they should look like, into ruling out anyone that does not fill that role. Some of the most successful searches can end by accepting a teacher who is totally different from what you expected. Conversely, you may be very disappointed in somebody who appears to fulfil your every requirement.

Instruction fees

The subject of teachers charging for their instruction is a contentious issue. Many people are understandably put off when they discover that they must get out their cheque books for the privilege of discovering what already lies within them. However, for the majority of organizations that teach meditation, a steady income is a practical necessity. Indeed, paying for teaching has been traditional practice for thousands of years, although payment may have been in the form of work, or service, rather than money. Even in the West, where the idea of paying for any kind of spiritual instruction seems quite alien, we need only look back to the tradition of paying tithes to the Church to recognize that there is nothing unusual about exchanging money for religious teaching.

The amount of money that you are prepared to pay is obviously a very important consideration, and you may still feel that charging for instruction in meditation is unacceptable. Some organizations, such as Transcendental Meditation (TM), have a sliding scale of fees, so that what you pay is directly related to your income. A teenager will be asked to pay a week's pocket money, whereas a bank manager's contribution would be greater. An undeniable benefit of paying for instruction is that people take seriously what they have had to pay for, and have a vested interest in getting their money's worth by giving the meditation technique a proper trial.

Working on your own

Finding the right teacher is no easy task and, although your progress may well be more rapid if you work with a qualified teacher, it is better to practise on your own than with the wrong teacher. Putting a great deal of energy into hunting for a teacher can be counterproductive and waste a lot of your time. In the natural course of things you will probably meet someone who can guide you when the time is ripe. You may actively prefer to work on your own. Many people feel uncomfortable about entrusting their meditation to somebody else, in which case working alone is a sensible and valid alternative.

Until or unless you find a teacher whom you find acceptable, much groundwork can be covered with the help of books, such as this, which provide practical guidelines and a range of techniques with which you can experiment to find the one best suited to your lifestyle and temperament. For those who prefer to work with a teacher within a traditional framework, the major spiritual traditions in which meditation is taught are now briefly described.

Christian mysticism

Although most people in the West are familiar with Christian teachings, its mystical element has been largely ignored. One reason for this may be that Christianity as an institution, as distinct from a spiritual path, has become so thoroughly assimilated into our society that it is commonly seen as little more than an advanced ethical code. Modern Christianity tends to emphasize the importance of performing good deeds and the avoidance of sin rather than the development of the individual, although a notable exception to this is the view held by 'born again' Christians, who maintain that Christianity is primarily about opening oneself up to the grace of God.

Christianity is, in fact, an essentially mystical religion – a way to God through Jesus Christ, the 'Word made flesh'. By guiding and initiating into the truth all those who seek by means of God's spiritual power, the Holy Spirit, Christ is himself the way to God. 'I am the way, and the truth, and the light,' he told his disciples. 'No one comes to the Father except through me.' (John 14:6) The Christian mystic seeks to be united with God through following the way of Christ.

Just as there are many varieties of Christianity, there are many different forms of contemplation practised by Christians, ranging from reflection on Biblical passages to meditation techniques which are virtually identical to some of those found in the traditions of the East. However, like all other mystics, those within the Christian tradition maintain that God can never be revealed through the intellect. As St Augustine put it, 'There is in the mind no knowledge of God except that it does not know Him.' Thus the most mystical forms of Christian contemplation go beyond conscious thought to a state of awareness similar to that cultivated in, for example, Zen. Described by the Spanish mystic St Teresa of Avila as 'the suspension of all internal and external powers', two principal routes – the *via positiva* and the *via negativa* – are offered as means to achieving this state.

The *via positiva*, or positive way, involves concentrating the mind on God's attributes – such as perfect love, goodness, and so on – in order to acquire a sense of God's magnitude. Through this kind of contemplation the Christian eventually transcends the limitations of conscious thought and becomes united with God in love and adoration. The *via negativa*, or negative way, is the more dominant path in the Christian mystical tradition and was strongly emphasized by Dionysius the Areopagite, a fifth-century Syrian monk whose writings have had enormous influence in Christian mysticism. Followers of this path seek knowledge of God by means of negation, by the non-attribution of any qualities – either positive or negative – to God. The reasoning behind this is that our ideas of qualities such as love or goodness are so limited that, in attributing these qualities to God, we are limiting Him to our own narrow concepts and breadth of experience. Only by leaving behind all ideas of God's attributes will the truth be revealed and the seeker be united with God. 'By not-seeing and by unknowing we attain to true vision and knowledge,' taught Dionysius.

Although Christian meditation is practised in many different forms, some of which are described in Chapter 4, running throughout the Christian mystical tradition is an emphasis on the mystical power of love. More important than the particular technique practised is the spirit in which the practice is undertaken – and this holds true for any form of meditation.

Taoism

'The universe is like Father Ocean, a stream of all things slowly moving. There is nothing to do but to maintain a true relationship to the things we move with and amongst and against.' Written not by a Chinese Taoist, but by the twentieth-century English novelist D. H. Lawrence, these words nevertheless contain the very essence of Taoist philosophy.

Philosophical Taoism, as distinct from much of the popular religious Taoism of today which is largely concerned with the pursuit of prolonged life and the acquisition of magical powers, was traditionally founded in the sixth or fifth century BC by Lao-tzu, author of the *Tao Te Ching*. The principles of the Tao, the underlying reality which pervades all existence, are beautifully expressed in *Tao Te Ching*, which reads as a series of observations about the world and our relationship to it.

The first lines of the *Tao Te Ching* establish at once that the Tao cannot be described: 'The Tao which can be spoken of is not the eternal Tao.' This is because it encompasses everything in the universe – it is both creative and destructive, both supportive and not supportive, both benevolent and malevolent. According to Taoism, every aspect of the universe has its counterpart, as seen in the relationship between light and dark, male and female, good and evil, hot and cold, and so on. These counterparts are called yin and yang, and are viewed as complementary, not opposed. Both yin and yang are intrinsic parts of one organic whole and the relationship between them is like that of the two sides of a coin, or the two poles of a magnet.

Taoism sees attempts to change the world from the outside as essentially futile. This does not mean that Taoism is in principle opposed to technology, nor that it preaches inaction and inertia, but that it views action as truly effective only when it is not forced. It is in this sense that the Taoist notion of non-action, or *wu-wei*, needs to be understood.

Wu-wei really means not going against the natural flow of things. This principle can be seen, for example, in the correct movement of the hands when catching a hard object such as a cricket ball. The movement of the hands follows the motion of the ball when catching it, thus reducing its impact and avoiding damage to the hands. Similarly, skyscrapers and suspension bridges must be designed to accommodate the wind, not resist it. Sailing, solar energy, working with the grain and gliding are all examples of *wu-wei* applied to familiar activities. Many artists have reported the feeling of their work emerging from the canvas, rather than being imposed on it from the outside. The composer Gustav Mahler had a similar experience when writing his third symphony: 'We do not compose,' he wrote, 'we are composed.'

Thus there is nothing inert or passive about *wu-wei*. Such activities are experienced as 'non-doing' because they follow the natural flow and are in accord with the Tao. The same is true of the Taoist concept of virtue, or *te*. *Te* does not mean virtue simply in the sense of morality; rather, it is the natural manifestation or expression of the Tao. True virtue is therefore not something we have to learn or be conscious of, but will arise from within of its own accord in the natural order of things.

As Taoism developed over the centuries, its principles were applied to the attempt to extend the natural lifespan, and yogic and alchemical practices were used for attaining longevity or even immortality. However Taoist meditation in its purer forms does not consider these as primary goals. In fact, the notion of extending one's life indefinitely is contrary to Taoist principles of yin and yang, since it is the certainty of death which gives life its value. Most Taoist meditation is designed to realign the mind and body with the Tao, and does not involve forcing of any kind.

Buddhism

Buddhism is the name given to the body of teachings ascribed to Siddhartha Gautama, the Buddha or 'enlightened one'. More a way of liberation than a religion, in that spiritual progress is achieved only through one's own efforts, Buddhism maintains that suffering is inherent in life and that the only way to end suffering is by ridding oneself of desire and delusion.

Since 400 years elapsed between the Buddha's death and the recording of his life and teachings, accounts vary. Different interpretations of the Buddha's teachings resulted in the development of various schools of Buddhism. The two main ones are the Theravada school, which dominates the southern half of the Buddhist world – Sri Lanka, Burma, Thailand, Cambodia and Laos, and the Mahayana school which is confined to the northern half – Nepal, Tibet, China, Korea and Japan. Although both schools have much in common – the Four Noble Truths and the eightfold path (see page 83), there are subtle differences in doctrine, practice and emphasis. For example, most Theravadins hold that enlightenment cannot be achieved in one lifetime, whereas many Mahayanists believe that this is possible, the latter being known as followers of the Sudden School. The emphasis in Mahayana is to strive for insight or enlightenment and, after realizing it, to return to the 'market place' – worldly life – and teach others. Such beings are called Boddhisattvas. Zen Buddhism, being less a spiritual philosophy than a means of experiencing the true nature of reality, has a distinctive flavour of its own and is discussed separately (see pages 83–85).

Born of a noble family in Nepal about 563 BC, Siddhartha Gautama led a privileged but sheltered life until the age of 29. One day, however, curious about the outside world, he asked to be driven through the city. Here, despite attempts to hide from him the old, the sick, the poor or people in any way miserable, Siddhartha saw a beggar, a sick man, a very old man, a corpse, and finally a wandering monk. On being questioned by Siddhartha, his charioteer admitted that misery and suffering were the lot of mankind, but that the monk had discarded worldly life and the pleasures of the senses, and instead sought the truth through austerities and meditation. Struck by this picture of human suffering, Siddhartha abandoned his home, wife and family, vowing to save not only himself but the whole of humanity from this universal experience of pain.

After six fruitless years as an ascetic, practising severe austerities, Siddhartha realized that he was still no nearer his goal. Breaking his fast, he accepted a bowl of curds from a young woman and then sat for meditation. He remained in the same posture under a banyan tree until, as dawn broke, he achieved full enlightenment, understanding both the reasons and the cure for human suffering.

Shortly after this, the Buddha or 'enlightened one' as he was henceforth known, preached his first sermon at a deer park near Benares. His philosophy was not new, but rather a restatement of Brahmin truths. In common with other Indian philosophies, Buddhism shares a belief in the doctrine of *karma* and reincarnation. According to the law of karma, every action we perform – and this includes thoughts and intentions – has its own fruit which, as the performer of that action, we experience. The same idea is found in other religions, such as Christianity – 'As you sow, so shall you reap.' However, in Indian philosophies this is tied to a belief in reincarnation, so that we experience the fruits of our actions sometimes in the present and sometimes in a future lifetime. According to this philosophy much of our experience in our present existence, for example where and into what kind of family or society we are born, is the result of our actions in a previous lifetime. Thus, through the operation of karma, we are trapped into a cycle of birth and death with all the suffering that this involves. We can be liberated from this endless round of life and death by following what is known as the Middle Way.

Having realized from experience the futility of both worldliness and extreme austerities, the Buddha taught the Middle Way, the way which lies between the two extremes of self-indulgence, which retards spiritual progress, and self-mortification, which is mentally and physically damaging. The Buddha's teachings are summed up in the Four Noble Truths:

1. The truth that human existence involves suffering – birth, ageing, sickness and death are all painful; association with what we dislike and separation from what we like is painful; not getting what we want is painful.
2. The truth that this suffering is caused by ignorance of what we truly are, which results in desire and in turn leads to rebirth.
3. The truth that suffering ends when desires cease, and we stop trying to grasp what is transitory. When desire is destroyed, we experience the Buddhist goal of *nirvana*.
4. The truth that we can put an end to suffering by following the Middle Way. This is an eightfold path which involves right understanding, right thought, right speech, right conduct, right means of livelihood, right effort, right mindfulness and right concentration.

Meditation is central to the practice of Biddhism, providing the strength to follow the eightfold path and leading to a disciplined mind and greater understanding. By dispelling ignorance and false identification with the ego, meditation is also a means by which *karma*, the consequences of past actions, can be obliterated. The ultimate goal of meditation is *nirvana*, the extinction of desire and delusion.

Zen Buddhism

Zen Buddhism developed as a result of the arrival of Buddhism in China, and its consequent exposure to, and shaping by, strong cultural influences, particularly Taoism. According to legend, Zen originated in the year 520 when Bodhidharma, the first patriarch, arrived from India and presented himself at the court of the Emperor Wu of Liang, a devout Buddhist. Asked by the Emperor what merit he had gained by building temples, copying scriptures and so on, Bodhidharma replied that no merit could be obtained from such deeds, which still showed worldly attachment, and that the only true merit was to be found in acts of pure wisdom that could not be understood by rational thought. Questioned about the holy absolute truth, Bodhidharma answered that truth is emptiness, and there is nothing in it to be holy. The Bodhidharma's doctrine and direct approach found little favour with the Emperor, so he left the court and spent several years in a monastery in the state of Wei, contemplating the wall. Later he communicated his teaching to Hui-k'o, who became the second patriarch.

It was not until the late twelfth century that Zen became established in Japan, although it was probably known there in the ninth century. Having taken root, however, it flourished and has made a great contribution to Japanese culture. Now increasingly popular in the West, Zen has nevertheless acquired a reputation for being highly esoteric and abstruse. In fact, Zen is one of the most direct and practical paths to mystical experience ever to have evolved. Better thought of as a way of liberation than a philosophy or religion, Zen is concerned with freeing our minds of concepts which prevent us from experiencing our true nature.

The word Zen, or Ch'an as it is called in China, comes from the Sanskrit *dhyana*, meaning simply meditation. In spite of the name, other Buddhist schools emphasize meditation as much as, or more than, Zen. What gives Zen its own particular character and distinguishes it from other forms of Buddhism are the way it views meditation, its direct methods of pointing to the truth, for example by means of *koans* (see pages 70–71), and its lack of reliance on the study of sacred texts. Dealing with practical realities rather than abstract concepts, Zen is 'learnt' in the way that a child learns to ride a bicycle – not by analysis or imitation, but by suddenly acquiring the 'knack'. To try to understand Zen intellectually is, in the words of one Zen master, to 'stink of Zen'.

The two main schools of Zen are the Soto and Rinzai schools. The practice of Rinzai Zen centres around the use of a *koan*, which is contemplated during meditation, whereas the form of meditation practised in Soto Zen often involves just sitting and nothing else (see *zazen*, page 69). The purpose behind both forms of meditation is identical. While the *koan* heightens awareness by breaking down logical, concept-bound ways of seeing the world, the practice of 'just sitting' cultivates a high level of awareness by focusing the mind on the present moment. In each case, meditation is concerned not with becoming something or acquiring wisdom, but simply with allowing the mind to reflect reality as it is, not as we habitually see it. The Zen experience of 'awakening', in which the nature of reality is perceived in its entirety, is known as satori.

Yoga

Yoga is a Sanskrit word related to the English 'yoke', and translates as 'union', as in the mystical experience of unity with God, and also as 'means' or 'method', as in spiritual discipline or application. Broadly speaking, yoga implies any spiritual path, but it is also the name of a particular school of Indian philosophy founded by Patanjali. The principles and practice of this philosophy are summarized in Patanjali's *Yoga Sutras*. Yoga is both a practical discipline and a philosophical system. According to Patanjali, it is only the activity of the mind which keeps us from awareness of our essential nature. The purpose of yoga is therefore to still the mind in order to experience the self, which is pure consciousness.

In its broader sense yoga covers any spiritual path by means of which enlightenment may be achieved, whether this is conceived of as the union of the individual soul with God, as the realization of one's own true nature or in some other way. The four classical forms of yoga are *hatha yoga*, which is the path to self-realization through purification of the physical body; *mantra yoga*, the path to self-realization through repetition of a sacred syllable, word or set of words; *raja yoga*, the path to self-realization through control of the mind using the system of Patanjali; and *laya yoga*, the path to self-realization through absorption of the mind in inner sounds and lights.

Yoga is also classified in terms of the different approaches to God described in the Hindu scriptures as *jñana yoga*, the path to self-realization through the intellect; *karma yoga*, the path to self-realization through selfless action; and *bhakti yoga*, the path to self-realization through devotion to God. Usually more than one form of yoga is practised as a means to enlightenment so an individual on the path of bhakti yoga may also repeat or chant the name of God as in mantra yoga, whilst performing all the actions with the feeling that God alone is the doer or actor, as in karma yoga.

The form of yoga most commonly practised in the West is hatha yoga and most areas have local classes. Another form of yoga in which there is increasing interest is kundalini yoga (pages 64–66 and 87). Meditation, which in this case generally involves focusing your attention on your breathing, a mantra or a visual object, plays an important part in most systems of yoga.

Hatha yoga

The aim of hatha yoga is the realization of one's own true nature through determined effort (*hatha* literally means 'force' or 'violence'), mainly through the practice of *asanas* (postures) and *pranayama* (breath control), which purify the body and allow the *prana* (breath of life, life force) to flow smoothly.

Most people in the West take up the practice of hatha yoga for health reasons and it is commonly thought that it deals solely with the physical body. In fact, although it does contribute to physical fitness, this yoga is primarily concerned with the flow of energy and the control of the mind. Another misconception is that hatha yoga is a preliminary to prepare the body for other 'higher' yogas. It is, in fact, a complete system and includes meditation.

Yoga is not just a daily practice. It is a way of life which requires the observance of certain rules of ethical conduct, *yama* and *niyama*, which are designed to purify the character and improve one's way of life. The seven stages of hatha yoga are *shodhana*, the cleansing of the body; *asana* or postures for strengthening and firming the body; *pranayama* or breath control; *mudra* or physical postures intended to stem the outward flow of the senses and turn the awareness inward; *pratyahara* or the withdrawal of the mind from the objects of the senses; *dhyana* or meditation; and finally *samadhi* or the state in which the unity or identity of the individual and the universal self is experienced. The first four stages deal with the body, whereas the final three have to do with the mind.

One of the aims of hatha yoga is to arouse the kundalini or divine energy. This is supposed to occur in the advanced stages of the practice as a result of performing certain *asanas* in combination with *mudras*, *bandhas* (postures in which certain parts of the body are contracted) and *pranayama*.

Kundalini yoga

Kundalini is a Sanskrit name for divine energy or creative power and is spoken of in one way or another in almost every language and tradition. In Japanese it is known as *ki*, in Chinese *chi* and in Christianity as the Holy Spirit. However the term *kundalini*, literally 'that which is coiled', usually refers to this power as it manifests itself in the human body. According to the *Tantras*, the Hindu sacred texts, the kundalini lies dormant in the subtle or psychic body in the *muladhara chakra* (a subtle energy centre whose approximate location in the physical body is at the base of the spine), in the form of a serpent coiled three and a half times.

When the kundalini is awakened, spiritual unfolding takes place and a process of transformation begins as it rises through the *sushumna* (the central energy channel in the subtle body) piercing the six *chakras* (energy centres) that lie on it. Impurities that block the flow of *prana* (life force) in the body and which are, according to yoga, the basis of all pain and disease, are expelled to allow the kundalini to do its work with full force. Physical and mental symptoms may appear as a result of this process. For example, an individual may temporarily become ill or suffer as latent diseases or anxieties are brought to the surface. Hallucinations, visions and other phenomena may be experienced as well as emotional states such as laughter or weeping. Spontaneous meditation occurs during which yogic processes such as breath retention or absorption in inner lights and sounds may occur, and some people are said to acquire supersensory powers such as clairvoyance or healing powers. Ultimately the kundalini becomes established in the *sahasrara*, at the crown of the head, at which point individual consciousness merges with divine or universal consciousness.

Several ways of awakening the kundalini are described in the Tantras and the practice of these systems is called kundalini yoga. This involves a combination of yogic techniques such as *pranayama* (breath control exercises), *asana* (postures), *mudra* (symbolic gestures) and concentration on the seven main *chakras*. These are meditated on individually, being visualized as lotuses with varying numbers of petals, each with its own deity (see page 65). Each chakra has particular qualities associated with it – specific vibrations, sounds, colours, elements and so on. However, many teachers of yoga have stressed the dangers of attempting to awaken the kundalini by such methods. If you succeed in awakening the kundalini through self-effort you will have certain experiences, but will still have to depend upon complicated yogic practices to lead the kundalini upwards. Few have the knowledge to accomplish this successfully and even for those who claim to have succeeded the experience can be a dangerous and terrifying one. In *Kundalini, The Evolutionary Energy in Man*, Gopi Krishna describes the upheavals and psychological disturbance he went through when kundalini awakening occurred as a result of many years' practice of yoga and meditation.

The safest and most effective way of awakening the kundalini is by means of initiation through a teacher whose own kundalini is fully activated. When the kundalini is awakened in this way it will ascend in the proper manner automatically and there is no danger involved.

Jewish mysticism

If the Jewish mystical tradition is perhaps less familiar than Zen or yoga, it is nonetheless a rich source of both holistic medicine and techniques of meditation. Jewish mystics recognized the connection between a person's state of mind and their physical condition hundreds of years ago, regarding health as a positive state of well-being in which a person not only enjoys physical health, but has a receptive mind and an underlying sense of purpose in life.

Mysticism has existed within Judaism since the early days, possibly originating with the esoteric teachings of sects such as the Essenes, four thousand years ago. But although it has its roots in earlier mystical traditions, the most important movement in the history of Jewish mysticism, known as the Kabbalah, did not become established until the thirteenth century.

The Kabbalah, which combines a highly developed and complex system of philosophy with specific techniques for increasing spiritual awareness, has had a chequered history. Originally confined to a small minority of Jews, Kabbalism went through a period of profound development as a result of the teachings of the influential Isaac Luria in the sixteenth century, and became a dominant force in the Judaic world. The seventeenth century, however, brought a decline in Kabbalistic teachings owing to a messianistic movement, which resulted in misinterpretation of its doctrines and consequent excesses, and the study of the Kabbalah became forbidden to all but a handful of scholars. During the eighteenth century Kabbalism again flourished in Eastern Europe, its teachings being widely spread through the Hassidic movement founded by Israel ben Eliezer, only to fall once more into disrepute with the rise of modern rationalist Judaism in the nineteenth century. Dismissed by this movement as mere speculation and medieval superstition, the Kabbalah has nevertheless begun to attract renewed interest in the late twentieth century and deserves as much attention as the teachings of any other great mystical tradition.

The essence of Kabbalistic teaching is that everything in the universe is derived from the same source, and that the purpose of existence is to recognize our identity with God and the whole of creation through spiritual practices such as meditation. Just as the Jewish people have lived in an almost constant state of exile from their homeland, so do we experience a continuous sense of exile from our own divine nature. However, the Kabbalah explains that 'exile contains redemption within itself, as seed contains the fruit'. This holistic, non-dual outlook is one of the most remarkable features of the Kabbalah. Just as Taoist philosophy expresses the interdependence of yin and yang, the Kabbalah views all the pairs of opposites – and indeed the entire universe – as interconnected.

Like other mystical traditions, the Kabbalah maintains that it is through stilling the mind that we can perceive our underlying nature. Great emphasis is placed on the importance of purifying the body, eating properly and meditating regularly. A number of different meditation techniques are available, but the particular technique chosen matters less in this tradition than the attitude and commitment of the meditator. Some meditations involve visualizing symbols such as the Tree of Life, which expresses the unity of creation. Others use the Hebrew alphabet to explore different permutations of the name of God. Each letter is considered to contain an aspect of the creative energy, so that by concentrating on the letters we become open to a state of awareness far beyond our normal, everyday consciousness. Another technique of meditation is to identify with the part of the mind which witnesses thought, and guided meditations are practised in order to confront tendencies such as anger, loneliness or hatred.

The ideal state of mind for meditation, common to all these

techniques, is one of focused attention or *kavvanah*. This involves the creation of a state of mind in which we are not subject to the limitations which conscious thought normally imposes on us. The Hassidic teacher Rabbi Dov Baer of Mezritch describes mystical experience and the process leading to it in the following words: 'When a man strips away the material aspect which envelops him, he will depict in his mind only the divine energy . . . so that its light will be of infinite greatness.'

Sufism

The Sufis are a mystic group generally associated with Islam. The origins of Sufism are uncertain – some claim that Sufism has always existed, others maintain that it developed from Islam, and yet others that it arose as a reaction against it. Although the large majority of Sufis are Muslim, and living in parts of the world where Islam is the dominant religion, the study and practice of Sufism does not necessarily involve embracing Islam. Western Sufism is non-Islamic from an orthodox point of view, and Sufi ideas are better thought of as a psychology than a religion.

There are hundreds of different Sufi orders, and the teachings and practices vary so much not only from one order to another, but within any particular order over the course of time, that it can appear that they have nothing whatever in common. Thus the study of Sufism may involve group recitation, dancing, fasts, the telling of stories, the observation of silence, meditation or a combination of any of these. The fact that Sufism *can* be taught in many different ways, and is continually evolving and adapting in response to the needs of the individual or the community at any given time, is a major feature of Sufism. Indeed, Sufis claim that it is only by constantly changing its external form that Sufism remains essentially the same.

What is common to all forms of Sufism is the aim – the transcending of limited thought processes and recognition of the reality which underlies appearances through the complete evolution of the individual, spiritually, physically and mentally. This is achieved through the interaction between the teacher and student, and between individual members of the community, rather than through the study of texts and acceptance of doctrine.

Thus Sufism is a supremely flexible system, perhaps more so than any other mystical tradition. The form it takes at any particular time depends on factors such as the culture within which it is practised and the personalities of individual students. Although a tradition of spiritual succession exists within Sufism, no Sufi methods or schools are set up as permanent institutions. A Sufi teacher may consider the continuation of particular teachings or forms of activity to be unnecessary or inappropriate after a certain time. A Sufi school may even disappear altogether, once having served the purpose for which it was established. What matters in Sufism, as in any other spiritual tradition, is not the form it takes, but the knowledge it engenders in those who follow it.

6

Questions and answers

Sooner or later everyone interested in meditation and spirituality is confronted with issues and questions which may concern either the actual experience during meditation or matters relating to the practice of meditation such as diet or personality changes. Some of the more common issues are discussed in this chapter, although it is only possible to give general guidelines. The answers invariably depend on the particular circumstances of the questioner and for this reason the same teacher will often answer the same question in different ways on different occasions. Some of the questions below have already been dealt with earlier, but because they are asked so frequently, they are briefly discussed again below. For a fuller discussion refer to the relevant chapter.

Physical discomfort during meditation

If you are unaccustomed to sitting still for any period of time you are likely to experience some discomfort when you first begin to meditate, sometimes so extreme as to make meditation almost impossible. Also, as most Westerners are unused to sitting in a cross-legged position, the traditional meditation postures may initially result in aching knees and backs. Fortunately meditation can, in fact, be practised in any position so long as the back and head are to be held straight, allowing the energy released during meditation to flow freely. However there are certain advantages attached to the traditional postures which make it worthwhile practising them if you are seriously interested in meditation and have reasonably flexible joints.

The lotus position, in which each foot is placed over the opposite thigh with the soles turned upwards, is a position of great balance and is also comfortable once mastered. The mind very naturally becomes quiet when you sit still for any length of time in this position, with the back and head held straight. If you practise the exercises given on pages 33–43 daily, within a few months you will be able to sit in the half lotus position, although it may take a year or two before you can sit in the full lotus. In the meantime, sit or lie for meditation in whatever position is most comfortable. Relax the body first with the techniques described on page 44. Repeat this during the meditation period if muscular pain and stiffness become a problem, and change positions if this helps.

Dealing with mental restlessness and streams of thought during meditation

Just as you can only see to the bottom of a lake if the water is still, and not muddy, you can only see and experience your own essential nature when the mind is clear. However, if the mind were already still there would be no need for meditation. Meditation is a means of stilling the 'waves' of the mind so that the truth is revealed.

There are many different approaches to dealing with the various thoughts and impressions that arise with great intensity at times during meditation. Attempting to drive them away is not usually successful, as illustrated by the story of the disciple who, at the time of his initiation, was told by his guru that he should never think of a black monkey just before meditating. The disciple saw no difficulty in this as he had no interest in monkeys and was therefore unlikely to think about them. The guru then whispered a mantra in the ear of the disciple and told him to go and meditate. Of course, as soon as the disciple sat down for meditation he remembered the guru's instruction and, sure enough, the image of a black monkey came straight into his head. The more he tried to get rid of it, the stronger the mental image became and eventually the disciple had to give up trying to meditate. The moral is, of course, that you should not impose conditions on meditation, nor try to deal with the mind by force.

Don't worry if thoughts arise in meditation. They won't do any harm. If you find them distracting, try one of these approaches.

1. Simply observe them, trying to discover where they come from and where they go.
2. Without trying to push them away, just bring your attention back to the breath or mantra or whatever kind of meditation you are practising.

Negative experiences and discouragement

As your practice of meditation progresses, deep-seated emotions and negativities can come to the surface of your consciousness and make you feel worse, not better. This is because meditation purifies the mind and body and, to do this thoroughly, all the 'junk' has to be thrown out. The process is a bit like spring-cleaning or clearing out cupboards. You come across all sorts of useless or outworn objects and garments, dirt and rubbish that you were completely unaware of. And in the process of clearing and sorting, everything seems to get in even more of a mess before things are finally straightened out. So also with meditation. But, as in the case of spring-cleaning, the best thing to do is keep going. You will only have wasted your time if you give up.

Tackle obsessions and feelings of anger, frustration, hate and so on in the same way as you do any thoughts and feelings that arise in meditation. Just as good or neutral thoughts can arise, so negative and even shocking impressions can surface during meditation, sooner or later to be completely expelled. Don't try to suppress them or judge them. Simply observe them or, if you like, immerse yourself in them and try to understand them. Find out where they come from and where they go to. In time they will subside. Again, the advice of a teacher who knows you personally and is aware of your circumstances can be of enormous help at this stage in your practice.

'Inability' to meditate

All you need to be able to meditate is the desire to do so. So long as you have sufficient interest in stilling the mind to practise one of the many methods which have been devised for the purpose, you will succeed. The feeling of 'inability' to meditate arises from imposing conditions on meditation and the experience you should be having. If, for example, you expect to have dramatic experiences during meditation, then you will be disappointed and feel unsuccessful if your experience does not match your expectations.

There is no such thing as 'right' experience in meditation. The only way to learn meditation is by practising it. Just follow the breath or repeat a mantra, or use any of the other techniques described in Chapter 4, and meditation will automatically take place. Sometimes it does feel as though nothing is happening, but you may be surprised to discover how differently you feel when you come out of meditation! You may well get bored, or feel that your mind wanders, but try to let go of your expectations and suspend judgement for a while. If you persevere you will certainly get results in the course of time. As with most things in life, the more you put in, the more you get out. Let whatever happens in meditation happen, and don't worry about it.

Drowsiness or sleeping during meditation

The mind is supposed to be alert and aware during meditation, so drowsiness in the sense of a dull mind and near-unconsciousness is not a state to be aimed for. However, some teachers maintain that the kind of sleep that you may fall into while absorbed in a mantra or other object of meditation, particularly if you remain in a sitting position, is beneficial. Schools of thought vary, though, and other teachers specifically advise keeping the eyes partially open to guard against falling asleep.

Taking a purely practical point of view, if you fall asleep during meditation it may simply be an indication that you are tired and need some rest. If this happens frequently when you meditate, try to find time to practise when you feel fresh and wide awake, and make sure you are getting enough sleep at night. If you are sleeping in meditation, but not as a result of tiredness, it is probably an indication that your mind has become still and, so long as you feel refreshed and energized as a result, there can certainly be no harm done. However, if you manage to stay alert and prevent yourself from falling asleep when your mind becomes quiet, you will fall into a state of deep meditation.

Is meditation selfish?

This is like asking 'Is prayer selfish?' or even 'Is playing sports selfish?' or 'Is studying for exams selfish?'. Nevertheless it is a question which is often asked. Different people meditate for different reasons – some for spiritual reasons, some to gain greater self-knowledge, some to relax a little and so on. Whatever the reasons may be, meditation is a means towards self-improvement, and those who persevere with it will find that they become more efficient in their everyday lives. This benefits not only the meditator, but those with whom he or she has contact. As a result of meditation a doctor will become a better doctor, an artist a better artist, and so on.

Obviously, if you choose to meditate at times when you should be doing other things, say helping out with the household chores, then you *are* being selfish. But in this case it is your approach to meditation that is selfish, not the practice of meditation itself. The practice of meditation should not mean neglecting day-to-day responsibilities. Set aside a convenient time to meditate and then carry out your practice without feeling guilty or that you could be spending your time more profitably doing something else. The stronger you become in yourself, the more you can really help and uplift others. If you have nothing yourself, then you can be of little help or use elsewhere and to others.

Is meditation escapist?

This question, like the last, comes down to a question of attitude. There is nothing intrinsically escapist about meditation, but if you use it as a means of withdrawal from the world to escape your problems or responsibilities, then you are doing it for the wrong reasons. Such behaviour tends to be self-defeating in any case. The roots of frustrations and problems lie within, and although you might obtain temporary relief by sitting in isolation meditating, sooner or later the same issues will arise and have to be dealt with. In the meantime a new set of problems has been created by the act of running away. The real goal of meditation is to remain inwardly peaceful and undisturbed even in the middle of people and worldly activities.

However there is nothing wrong with a temporary withdrawal from the world, for example to go on a retreat, or even going to live in a spiritual community, so long as this does not involve neglecting family or social responsibilities.

Does meditation involve a change of diet?

Generally speaking, the more you meditate, the more sensitive you become, both physically and mentally. In relation to food, this has the effect of helping you to become more aware of how your body is responding to what you eat. Therefore while meditation does not of itself involve a change of diet, you may, as a result of meditation, find that your eating habits change of their own accord.

As a general rule a light diet is best for meditation, and ideally you should wait a couple of hours after a light meal, and three or four after a heavy meal, before sitting for meditation. Eating wholefoods (foods which are unprocessed and free of additives, preservatives and artificial colouring), cutting down on fatty foods (meat, eggs and dairy products) and avoiding too many stimulants (such as the caffeine in tea and coffee) will all put less strain on your body and make your meditation easier. Some teachers prefer a vegetarian diet as being the lightest and at the same time nutritious, balanced, healthy and inexpensive. However it is certainly not necessary to become a vegetarian in order to practise meditation.

Does the use of mind-altering drugs interfere with meditation?

As explained above, the practice of meditation results in increased sensitivity, so the effects of mind-altering drugs can be heightened as a result, even outside the actual period of meditation. Meditation is a powerful means of altering consciousness, so reinforcing it with drugs while you are meditating can be very dangerous indeed.

Your progress in meditation will certainly be hindered by the use of powerful drugs. However studies undertaken in America indicate that, with the regular practice of meditation, people with a drug habit tend to lose their dependency. Meditation is increasingly being seen as an effective tool in the treatment of drug addiction and alcoholism.

Does meditation involve changing one's lifestyle?

Besides maintaining the discipline of setting aside a regular period of time to meditate, and being in a fit state to do it – in other words not too tired or too full of food, not drunk or under the influence of other mind-altering drugs – meditation does not involve any change of lifestyle. Lifestyle changes frequently ensue, however, as a result of meditation. Bad habits like smoking or excessive drinking often diminish. As discussed above, some meditators, as they become more sensitive and aware of the way foods affect them, may make changes in their diet. A more orderly and simple lifestyle may be adopted.

As a result of meditation, you may find yourself making

beneficial changes in lifestyle in a spontaneous and natural fashion. But there is no need to force anything. If you become a fanatic teetotaller overnight, or suddenly insist on eating nothing but organic bean sprouts, your only achievement will be to alienate family and friends. And the more fanatical you become, the more resistance you will encounter. The important thing is to maintain a sense of balance and to use your common sense.

Will meditation alter my personality?

Some people worry, especially after reading accounts of mystical experience, that their personality might become submerged as a result of meditation. It is true that all sense of 'I' and 'mine' dissolves during mystical experience, but this does not in any way mean that the mystic loses his or her individual personality. On the contrary, descriptions of mystics throughout history indicate that they have very definite, very alive personalities, and are frequently highly practical and efficient in the way they conduct their day-to-day affairs, as well.

Asking whether meditation will change your personality is analogous to asking if psychotherapy will change your personality. Both aim for increased self-knowledge and personal growth, and for any real growth to take place – whether or not you happen to meditate – there must be change of some kind. But rather than changing your personality, meditation subtly refines and strengthens it. The process of meditation helps you to recognize and discard the various false fronts and layers of anxiety or prejudice through which you confront the world, so that your real self can shine through. As a result your inner experience – the way you understand and feel about things – will change, and your outer behaviour and goals will reflect this.

Should teachers of meditation charge for instruction?

Some spiritual traditions regard money as dirty, as do some spiritual seekers, who are immediately put off if a donation is requested. However, the fact that a teacher does not charge for instruction does not mean that he or she can automatically be trusted – unscrupulous teachers can exploit their students in less obvious ways. A small donation for instruction is a perfectly reasonable request – money is a basic necessity of life and naturally any teacher or organization needs to pay for their premises and other necessary items.

On the other hand, you should be wary if a teacher or organization is operating as a big business. If you are happy to pay out a large proportion of your hard-earned money for the privilege of attending a spiritual centre, only to spend half your time there doing all their washing up, there are plenty of organizations who will welcome you with open arms. This really can happen! However there are also plenty of organizations who operate on a different basis, and money certainly doesn't buy cosmic consciousness.

Is meditation a form of hypnosis?

Hypnosis is a form of trance in which the subject is in a highly suggestible state. Meditation is *not* a form of trance. It is a state of full awareness in which the question of modifying behaviour in accordance with suggestions and instructions that the conscious self would block does not arise. (Refer back to page 00 for a fuller discussion.)

Does meditation involve adopting specific beliefs or value systems?

Meditation can be practised either in a secular or religious context and it does not in any way require acceptance of a set of beliefs. On the contrary, meditation should be approached with an open mind, and all beliefs and concepts set aside as far as possible during the actual period of practice. (Refer back to page 17 for a fuller discussion.)

How can you judge progress in meditation?

The quality of your meditation and, more importantly, your inner development, are indications of your progress in meditation. However, personal evolution is a gradual process and you should not expect immediate results.

In the initial stages of meditation the beneficial effects are often felt mainly on a physical level – a feeling of deep relaxation and general well-being. As meditation deepens and the psychological effects begin to occur, meditators can go through difficult periods and may feel not only that they are making no headway, but that they are actually losing ground.

Internal growth and development is a slow process and it involves change, which can be painful. Prepare for difficult times and don't judge your progress from day to day. In the long term you can judge your progress in meditation by, for example, whether or not you have developed greater insight, sensitivity and personal power; whether or not you are more emotionally stable; how calm you remain in difficult circumstances; how much inner peace and satisfaction you experience.

Visions, strange physical sensations and other psychic phenomena

Visions, inner lights and sounds, clairvoyance, out-of-the-body experiences and so on are not uncommon experiences in meditation. They are normal reactions and should be treated in much the same way as thoughts and desires which arise in meditation. In other words, don't pay too much attention to them.

Involuntary physical movements and other strange physiological phenomena can occur as a result of the process of purification triggered off by meditation. By this process physical and mental impurities are eliminated, enabling spiritual energy to flow freely. Visions sometimes serve as a signpost and encourage the meditator to continue the practice. However, if you allow such phenomena to become goals in themselves they will only serve to hinder your progress. The real attainment is the direct experience of ultimate reality, which is without shape or form, and teachers of all traditions have warned against confusing psychic and paranormal phenomena of this kind with genuine mystic experience.

If phenomena of a disturbing nature occur repeatedly you should discontinue your practice and seek the advice of an experienced teacher of meditation.

Reference section

This section is designed to give you an idea of the range of organizations and individuals teaching meditation. It is not intended to be exhaustive or comprehensive, nor should it be read as 'the good meditation guide'! Where appropriate, teachers have been listed under the traditions they represent, as outlined in Chapter 5, and there is a general section for organizations which are not affiliated to any particular tradition.

It should be noted that the omission of a name does not necessarily mean that they cannot be recommended. Conversely, the quality of teaching within any of the groups listed may vary from time to time, and it is generally advisable to carry out your own assessment before committing yourself. If you wish to find out objective information about a spiritual organization, you may wish to approach INFORM, an independent charity based at the London School of Economics. They can be contacted at:

INFORM
Houghton Street
London WC2A 2AE
Tel. 020 7955 7654
Email. inform@lse.ac.uk
www.inform.ac

Where possible, international addresses of large organizations have been given, but if you live outside the United Kingdom, local libraries might be able to help you find a meditation centre in your area. Teachers who do not charge for instruction are indicated.

Finding a Teacher

The best way of finding a meditation teacher in your area is by word of mouth, by looking at the notice boards in libraries, wholefood shops, bookshops and universities, or by searching the internet. Meditation websites of interest include:

Meditation Sites

TM (Transcendental Meditation)

www.tm-london.org.uk
No-nonsense introduction stressing the practical benefits of TM (see also pp 106-7) and useful contact addresses.

Samatha Meditation

www.samatha.demon.co.uk
Samatha meditation technique has its roots in the Thai Theravadin tradition, and was introduced to England in 1962 by a Thai meditation teacher. The Samatha Trust was formed in 1973 to support the teaching of this form of meditation practice in various parts of the country and to establish a national centre. It has also published a number of works on Buddhist theory and practice.

www.meditation-lessons.com
An introduction to meditation with a course available on the internet

Vipassana Meditation

www.nandawon.demon.co.uk/meditate.htm
An interesting page on this Burmese tradition and its work in prisons

Buddhist Sites

www.londonbuddhistvihara.co.uk/meditation.htm

www.aukana.org.uk/amed.html
Website for The House of Inner Tranquillity, a meditation centre which was established for those in search of a practical approach to the Buddha's path. Under the spiritual guidance of Alan James, who co-founded the centre in 1980, it offers comprehensive instruction in the course of training as laid down in the Pali Canon (the collection of the Buddha's original discourses). Situated in the centre of the market town of Bradford on Avon,

the meditation centre is an extensive property (formerly a school) containing over a dozen bedrooms, offices, a library and a spacious shrine room, all set in a couple of acres of gardens.

Also recommended are the following journals:

Resurgence

Editorial Dept.
Ford House
Hartland
Nr. Bideford
Devon EX39 6EE
Tel. 01237 441293
Fax. 01237 441203
Email: ed@resurge.demon.co.uk

Sufi

41 Chepstow Place
London W2 4TS
Tel. 020 7221 1129
Tel./Fax. 020 7229 0769
Email: Alireza@sufism.demon.co.uk
www.nimatullali.org

Published quarterly

Tricycle and *Buddhism Now*

Buddhist Publishing Group
Sharpham Coach Yard
Ashprington
Totnes
Devon TQ9 7UT
Tel. 01803 732082 and 01803 864009

Yoga & Health

P.O. Box 29
Brighton BN1 8JQ
Tel. 01273 563111
Email: fotodirect@mistral.co.uk
www.yogaandhealthmag.com

Useful addresses

Yoga

Iyengar Yoga

B.K.S. Iyengar is one of the world's foremost exponents of hatha yoga and classes using the Iyengar approach are widely available throughout the UK. For information and details of classes and courses contact:

Iyengar Yoga Institute
223a Randolph Avenue
London W9 1NL
Tel. 020 7624 3080
Fax. 020 7372 2726
Email: office@iyi.org.uk
www.iyi.org.uk

Self-Realization Fellowship

This movement was founded by Paramhansa Yogananda, the author of *Autobiography of a Yogi*. Yogananda was one of the first teachers to come to the West (1920), where he taught for over 30 years. He died in 1953, but his work is carried on by former students. Meetings are held each week in the Notting Hill and Hampstead areas of London, details of which are available on 020 7286 1524, or on their website www.yogananda-srf.org.

Siddha Yoga

Yoga tradition whose spiritual head is currently Gurumayi Chidvilasananda. This tradition offers meditation, including the use of mantra and breathing techniques, but is rooted in spiritual initiation, in which the guru plays an essential part. There are centres worldwide and throughout the UK, addresses available from:

SYDUK
32 Cubitt Street
London WC1X 0LR
Tel. 020 7278 0035
www.siddhayoga.org

Sivananda Yoga Vedanta Centre

The Sivananda Yoga Vedanta Centre was founded by Swami Vishnu Devananda, a student of the late Swami Sivananda. The centre offers courses in meditation at three levels, including instruction in posture, concentration, mantras, philosophy, and a study of Patanjali's *Yoga sutras*. Although the centre charges for its courses, there are special arrangements for people with financial difficulties. The centre also organizes retreats.

The Sivananda Yoga Vedanta Centre
51 Felsham Road
Putney
London SW15 1AZ
Tel. 020 8780 0160
Fax. 020 8780 0128
Email: siva@dial.pipex.com

Buddhism

There are hundreds of Buddhist groups operating in the UK, and this list is restricted to some of those which offer courses in meditation. The Buddhist Society, London, publishes *The Buddhist Directory*, which lists Buddhist and Zen centres and groups in the UK and Ireland. This should be consulted if you wish to establish contact with a group in your area.

The Buddhist Society
58 Eccleston Square
London SW1V 1PH
Tel. 020 7834 5858
Email: info@thebuddhistsociety.org.uk
www.thebuddhistsociety.org.uk

The Buddhist Society was founded in 1924 by Christmas Humphreys QC with the aim to 'publish and make known the principles of Buddhism and to encourage the study and application of those principles'. It does not adhere to any one school of Buddhism, and is wholly impartial in its teaching. There is also a quarterly journal, *The Middle Way*.

Tibetan Buddhism

Rigpa
330 Caledonian Road
London N1 1BB
Tel. 020 7700 0185
Fax. 020 7609 6068
Email: 114335.615@compuserve.com
Rigpa UK Website: www.rigpa.fsnet.co.uk
International Buddhist organisation based on the teachings of Sogyal Rinpoche. Tibetan Buddhist and bestselling author of *The Tibetan Book of Living and Dying*. Rigpa offers courses of study and practice, and introductory programmes of meditation.

Zen

Dr Ad Brugman and Sonia Moriceau
The Orchard
Lower-Mascoed
Hereford HR2 0HP
Tel. 01873 860207
Dr Brugman and Sonia Moriceau offer 3- and 5-day workshops in outdoor activities.

Bristol Ch'an Group
c/o Tim Blanc
29 Gwillilm Street
Windmill Hill
Bristol BS3 4LT
Tel. 0117 909 8528

Western Zen Retreats
c/o Tim Blanc
29 Gwillilm Street
Windmill Hill
Bristol BS3 4LT
Tel. 0117 909 8528
These retreats are held every five or six weeks, and involve the practice of zazen and communication exercises. The basic teaching is Soto Zen. Contact Dr. John Crook at the above address. Retreats are held in association with the Bristol Ch'an Group.

Throssel Hole Priory
Carrshield
Hexham
Northumberland NE47 8AL
Tel. 01434 345204

This is a monastery following the Soto Zen tradition. Guests are welcome, and can contact the Guestmaster at the above address. The monastery is also affiliated to the Manchester Zen Group, who may be contacted on (0161) 872 2879.

Jewish mysticism

Z'ev ben Shimon Halevi (Warren Kenton)
Way of Kabbalah Courses
Flat 2
31-33 Priory Park Road
London NW6 7UP
Tel. and Fax. 020 7625 9537

Warren Kenton spent over thirty years studying Kabbalah in Europe, Israel and North Africa. He has published eleven books on Kabbalah, and runs weekend and residential summer courses. He also produces meditation tapes. He lives and works in London with his wife.

Sufism

Nimatullahi Sufi Order
41 Chepstow Place
London W2 4TS
Tel. 020 7229 0769

The Nimatullahi Sufi Order has centres in Western Europe, Australia, Africa and North America. It publishes the quarterly journal *Sufi*.

Transcendental meditation

Transcendental Meditation, or TM, is probably the largest organization teaching meditation in the world, with about 80 teaching centres in the UK alone.

TM is a mantra-based technique which is easily learnt and

very effective. Learning TM is not cheap, however. It costs in the region of £500 for a four-session course, though reduced fees may be negotiated on the basis of need.

For a free information pack and details of your nearest centre contact:

National Enquiries Office
Beacon House
Willow Walk
Skelmersdale
Lancashire WN8 6UR
Tel. 08705 143733
www.t-m.org.uk

General and centres for retreats

The Good Retreat Guide by Stafford Whiteaker, updated regularly and published by Rider (first edition, 1991), is an excellent book on where to go for retreats.

Gaia House
West Ogwell
Newton Abbot
Devon TQ12 6DY
Email. gaiahouse@gn.apc.org

Gaia House is a meditation centre with visiting teachers from different traditions. A programme of courses is available on request.

Life Foundation International Course Centre
Nant Ffrancon
Bethesda
Bangor
Gwynedd LL57 2EG
Tel. 01248 602900
Fax. 01248 602004
Email. enquiries@lifefoundation.org.uk

Lendrick Lodge
Brig o'Turk
Callander
Perthshire
Scotland
Tel. 0187 76263

The Life Foundation of Therapeutics and Lendrick Lodge both specialize in yoga and t'ai chi courses.

The Barn
Lower Sharpham Barton
Ashprington
Totnes
Devon TQ9 7DX
Tel. 01803 732661
Email. sharphambarn@dial.pipex.com
The Barn specializes in retreats based on yoga and Buddhism.

Tapes for meditation

There is an increasing number of tapes available which have been specially designed for meditation. A large range is available from:

New World Music
16a Neals Yard
Covent Garden
London WC2H 9DP
Tel. 020 7379 5972
New World Music is a friendly shop, equipped with listening facilities. All their tapes are listed under such headings as visualization, meditation, anti-stress, and so on. They also provide a mail order service.

Further reading

General

James, W., *The Varieties of Religious Experience*, Penguin, 1983
Leshan, L., *How to Meditate*, Little, Brown and Company, 1999
Rinpoche, S., *Meditation*, Rider Books, 2001
Underhill, E., *Mysticism*, Oneworld Publications, 1999
Zaehner, R.C. (ed.), *The Concise Encyclopaedia of Living Faiths*, Hutchinson, 1997

Yoga

Eliade, M., *Yoga*, Princeton University Press, 1970
Hewitt, J., *The Complete Book of Yoga*, Rider Books, 1987
Paramahansa, *Autobiography of a Yogi*, Rider Books, 1996
Stoler Miller, B. (Trans.), *Yoga: Discipline of Freedom: The Yoga Sutra Attributed to Patanjali*, Bantam Books, 1998

Hatha yoga

B. K. S. Iyengar, *Light on Yoga*, HarperCollins, 2001
B. K. S. Iyengar, *Yoga: the Path to Holistic Health*, Dorling Kindersley, 2001
Devereux, G. *Hatha Yoga*, HarperCollins, 2001
Sivananda Yoga Centre, *The New Book of Yoga*, Ebury Press, 2000

Kundalini yoga

Avalon, A. (Sir John Woodroffe), *The Serpent Power*, Dover Publications, 1974
Kaur Khalsa, Shakta, *Kundalini Yoga*, Dorling Kindersley, 2001
Muktananda, Swami, *Play of Consciousness*, Harper & Row, 1978

Tantrism

Evans-Wentz, W. (ed.), *The Tibetan Book of the Dead*, OUP, 2000
Rinpoche, S., *The Tibetan Book of Living and Dying*, Rider Books, 1998

Taoism

Cleary, T., *Taoist Meditation*, Shambhala, 2000
Forstater, M., *The Spiritual Teachings of the Tao*, Hodder & Stoughton, 2001
Hoff, B., *The Tao of Pooh*, Methuen, 1998
Mitchell, S., *Tao Te Ching*, Frances Lincoln, 1999

Buddhism

Batchelor, S., *Buddhism Without Beliefs*, Bloomsbury, 1998
Dalai Lama, *Transforming the Mind*, Harper Collins, 2000
Causton, R., *The Buddha in Daily Life*, Rider Books, 1995
Lama Surya Das, *Awakening the Buddha Within*, Bantam, 1997
Pym, J., *You Don't Have to Sit on the Floor*, Rider Books, 2001
Snelling, J., *The Buddhist Handbook*, Rider Books, 1998

Zen Buddhism

Herrigal, E., *Zen and the Art of Archery*, Arkana, 1990
Kapleau, R. P., *The Three Pillars of Zen*, Doubleday, 1989
Reps, P. (Ed.), *Zen Flesh, Zen Bones*, Penguin, 2000
Watts, A., *The Way of Zen*, Arkana, 1990

Jewish mystical tradition

Abelson, J., *Jewish Mysticism*, Dover Publications, 2001
Besserman, P., *The Shambhala Guide to Kabbalah and Jewish Mysticism*, Shambhala Publications, 1998
Cohn-Sherbok, D., *Jewish Mysticism*, Oneworld, 1995

Christian mystical tradition

Merton, T., *Contemplative Prayer*, Darton, Longman & Todd, 1973

Underhill, E., *The Cloud of Unknowing*, R A Kessinger Publishing, 1998

Witkam, J., *The Eye Aware*, Lantern Books, 2001

Sufism

Arabi, I., *The Seven Days of the Heart*, Anqa Publishing, 2000

Lewisohn, L., *The Wisdom of Sufism*, Oneworld, 2001

Shah, I., *Learning How to Learn*, Arkana, 1993

Shah, I., *The Way of the Sufi*, Arkana, 1990

Tweedie, I., *Daughter of Fire*, The Golden Sufi Centre, 1995

Index